Joseph Cawthorne

A letter to the king

In Justification of a Pamphlet, Entitled

Joseph Cawthorne

A letter to the king
In Justification of a Pamphlet, Entitled

ISBN/EAN: 9783744763981

Printed in Europe, USA, Canada, Australia, Japan

Cover: Foto ©Suzi / pixelio.de

More available books at **www.hansebooks.com**

A LETTER

TO THE

K I N G,

IN

JUSTIFICATION OF A PAMPHLET,

ENTITLED,

"THOUGHTS

ON THE

ENGLISH GOVERNMENT."

A LETTER

TO THE

KING,

IN

JUSTIFICATION of a PAMPHLET,

ENTITLED,

"THOUGHTS

ON THE

ENGLISH GOVERNMENT:"

WITH

AN APPENDIX

IN ANSWER

To Mr. FOX's

DECLARATION of the WHIG-CLUB.

———————

London:

PRINTED FOR THE AUTHOR;

AND

SOLD BY J. OWEN, N. 168, PICCADILLY.

[*Price 2s. 6d.*]

———

1796.

TO THE

K I N G.

THE production which I prefume, with the greateſt humility, to lay at your Majeſty's Feet, has a modeſt claim to the Royal Ear, becauſe it treats upon a ſubjeƈt which is extremely intereſting to your Majeſty's Government, at a period in which there ſeems to be a plot to undermine every Monarchical Government, and indeed to new model every Government upon the chaotic ſyſtem of the French rebellion. As your reign

b   has,

has, without a fingle exception, difcovered the fineft difpofition and the firmeft
refolution to promote, not only the happinefs of your Subjects, as the true dignity of the Throne, but the rights and
fecurity of Europe; it might reafonably
have been expected that the happy Government of a Monarch fo amiable and
fo juft to all the world, would have
efcaped the pretence which is found for
the fubverfion of the worft Governments:
But, fuch is the phrenfy of the times,
that no diftinction is made between the
good and the bad; for, like the contagion
of the body natural, the beft and the
worft are brought to a level upon a principle of EQUALITY, which deftroys the
beautiful order of things and endangers
every thing dear to fociety.

Befides this general claim to the con-
defcenfion of my Gracious Sovereign (a
claim

claim now wifely admitted by the moſt abſolute Monarchs) I have a particular title to your Majeſty's attention, from an event that places your Majeſty in an aukward ſituation: I mean, SIRE, the motion of one of your principal Secretaries of State, adopted by the Houſe of Commons, to proſecute one of your Majeſty's beſt ſubjects, not for violating any law or injuring any authority, but for a publication that manifeſtly promotes principles of ſubordination which have rendered the moſt eminent ſervices to your Majeſty's Government. That very Miniſter has candidly acknowledged, that " The Nation owes the peace and ſecu- " rity it now enjoys to the diſtinguiſhed " ſervices of the Author;" and yet, with a ſtrange ſort of conſiſtency, the Secretary of State moved the Houſe of Commons to addreſs your Majeſty to direct a proſecution againſt him for a Pamphlet that

b 2   maintains

maintains the principles which have produced that great event at the moft alarming period. Such an application to the Throne is, by the Minifter's own confeffion, an act of great injuftice to fo meritorious a fubject, and a great indignity to your Majefty's reign: It is, in my humble opinion, a cruel injuftice to a fubject fo eminently diftinguifhed for his fervices at the worft period, and as great an injuftice to the illuftrious character of your Majefty, which is as much the admiration of Foreigners as it is the pride of your Subjects.

A Monarch fo well acquainted with the conftitution of his kingdom, and fo religioufly attached to it, will immediately difcover that your Majefty has no right to direct fuch a profecution, nor the Houfe of Commons any right to require it. If the Author has violated any Law,

or

or is fuppofed to be guilty of a Libel on
the Conftitution, your Majefty has no
right to interfere. Your Government
and the Laws of the Land are competent
without the Royal interpofition: Executive Government can, in the latter cafe,
proceed without your Majefty's inter-
ference.

Having prefumed to fay fo much in
defence of an Author that I very much
admire, and to whofe eminent fervices
one of your Majefty's principal Secretaries
of State bears the moft honorable tefti-
mony, by declaring that, in his opinion,
" The Public owe the peace and fecurity
" they now enjoy to him;" I may now
venture, with the moft dutiful zeal for
your Majefty's Government, to fay a
word on the temper of the times, and
the fpirit of political contagion that pervades Europe, and which, making no
diftinction,

diftinction, endangers the beft as well as the worft Government.

But before I come to that interefting fituation of things, I will take a tranfient view of your Majefty's reign. A fpirit of party is interwoven with the Conftitution, and infeparable from it. Oppofition is the natural and indeed the neceffary effect of a mixed Government: It is effential to a limited Monarchy: And if it exceeds the bounds of reafon, it is a fpeck in the eye of the Conftitution, which fhould be touched with a trembling hand. There have been two memorable periods in your Majefty's reign, in which the fpirit of Party has exceeded its ufual bounds: One during the unfortunate American war; and the other in the prefent war with the French Revolution. Both thefe events I fhall defend in a few words upon principles of

inevitable

inevitable neceffity. All wars are in their nature calamitous, and to be avoided as a fcourge to mankind; but, in thefe inftances, they are juftifiable as being inevitable. Such was the cafe of the American war; and fuch is abfolutely the prefent cafe. The faithful hiftorian will place thefe wars in a light that will do juftice to your Majefty's reign: He will judge of them by their principles, and not by their fuccefs. The principle of the American war was juft, though the end was unfortunate: No one will difpute the right of this Nation to contend for the prefervation of her American Colonies, which were of fo much value to a trading Nation. If an ineffectual ftruggle rendered it unpopular, it was occafioned, in a great meafure, by the treachery of domeftic foes who infifted on their emancipation, and the facrifice of fo valuable a part of your Majefty's dominions. That war

was

was conducted by one of the beft Minifters of Europe: A Minifter, who was
an honor to human nature. The noble
Lord poffeffed one of the ableft heads
and beft hearts in the kingdom. His
talents and his virtues would do honor
to any State and to any Age. Such was
the character of Lord North, whofe
memory will be highly refpected when
the malice of his political enemies is
forgotten, and the motives that gave it
birth.

The prefent war with France is founded on the fame principle of abfolute neceffity. To the honor of your Majefty's
reign, you have manifeftly been forced
into wars againft the ftrongeft difpofition
to preferve the Tranquillity of Europe,
and the Balance of Power; in order that
a check to the ambition of the ftrongeft,
may be a fecurity to the weakeft ftate.
The

(ix)

The ambition of conqueſt has never influenced your Majeſty's conduct. The love
of mankind, and of ſubſtantial juſtice to
promote a juſt *equilibrium*, has ever been
your Majeſty's ruling paſſion, and the
great objects of your reign. It has indeed been ſaid, that the preſent war is
equally unjuſt and unfortunate: But I
contend that, whatever may be the ſuc-
ceſs, the principle is juſt and neceſſary.
Should it be ſaid that this Nation might
have avoided it, and that Great Britain
was the aggreſſor, I take the liberty to
deny both. The Revolution of France
rendered a war with this county inevitable, ſince the principles of that Revolution, were a declaration of war againſt
every other Government. The aggreſ-
ſion was not in the firſt open act but
in the principles of hoſtility againſt all
Europe, and a mad ambition to ſubvert
every Government. There was no avoid-

c   ing

ing a defence againſt ſuch a political contagion, that has convulſed and nearly overthrown all Europe. Never was a war conducted upon better principles to preſerve the Government and intereſt of this Nation, and the ſecurity of all other European States.

 The ſecurity of Holland alone, was ſufficient to juſtify the preſent war; and ſhould it be ſaid that object was once obtained, and that it was then time to make peace, I deny it; becauſe there was no ſecurity for its preſervation in the principles of the French unſettled Government. Whatever has been the loſs of blood and treaſure to this Nation, the juſtice of the war is clearly on the ſide of your Majeſty's Government: And whenever your Majeſty ſhall obtain the *Status quo* to reſtore the balance of power in Europe, your Majeſty, even without

any

any compenfation, will make a glorious
Peace by the greateft acquifition,—the
fecurity of your dominions, which is invaluable. This fhews that the prefent
war is juft and neceffary, for without it
this Nation and all Europe, would probably have been in the dreadful fituation
of France, without the power perhaps
of recovering their dominions, their peace,
and their property.

Confidering then how great might
have been the lofs to this country and
all Europe without a war, from the contagion of levelling principles, that war
will be glorious, whatever may be the
expence of blood and treafure, which
procures a folid peace founded on the
general intereft and fecurity of Europe,
which have ever been the great objects
of your Majefty's reign.

Having,

Having, with as much precifion as poffible, juftified the foreign fyftem of your Majefty, I fhall now prefume to fpeak of your domeftic Government, which I equally admire. The principles which pervaded France could not fail of infecting this country, and fo ftrong has been the infection, and fo alarming the confequences, that it would probably have overthrown this Government as it has done that, but for your Majefty's wifdom. Strong meafures have been found neceffary, but nothing can be too ftrong to preferve the Peace and Property of the Kingdom. How fortunate would it have been, had fuch preventive meafures been taken prior to the fhameful riots of 1780, which difgraced your Majefty's Government, and threatened the very exiftence of the Nation.

Of the profecutions for *fictitious* treafon

I am

I am fure your Majefty ever rejoices at
the acquittal of your fubjects by the
Laws of the Land: A Sovereign eminently diftinguifhed for clemency and
for all the virtues that adorn a Throne,
is ever pleafed at their reftoration to
fociety. The Bill againft Sedition has
been greatly mifreprefented: The principle is excellent, and the operation of the
Act will effectually deftroy the contagion
of revolutionary principles, and preferve
the dignity of authority, and the tranquillity and property of the public, which
without the fecurity of that well-judged
and well-timed meafure, would all be
abforbed in the vortex of anarchy and
confufion.

What has therefore been done from
neceffity, the greateft of all Laws, to
preferve the public peace from the terror of public incendiaries, has been well
done

done and well-timed, and I think cannot
fail of producing the happieft effects
without thofe abufes of power, with
which fome men have alarmed the weak,
and armed the reftlefs againft the neceffary meafures of your Majefty's Government. I am fo well perfuaded that all
oppofition to ftrong but neceffary meafures will foon ceafe, and that they will
effectually fupprefs the confpiracy of
mifguided men againft the authorities of
the State, and the true intereft and happinefs of your Majefty's fubjects, that I
venture to anticipate my moft humble
congratulations to the Throne.

To witnefs this happy, this glorious
event, by the reftoration of good order
and perfect fecurity, I moft fervently
pray to the Almighty that your Majefty
may long, very long, enjoy health and
every bleffing that Heaven can beftow!

With

(xv)

With this true loyalty, and fincere
devotion, I have the happinefs to be,

S I, R E,.

Your Majefty's moft dutiful,

And moft faithful Subject,

JOSEPH CAWTHORNE.

Greenwich Park,
December 26, 1795.

Your M[ajesty's] most devoted,

And most faithful Subject,

JOSEPH CAWTHORN.

A

JUSTIFICATION

OF THE

AUTHOR OF A PAMPHLET,

INTITLED,

" *THOUGHTS ON THE ENGLISH*

GOVERNMENT."

Unfit I follow, where *he* led the way,
And court applaufe, by what I feem to pay.
Myfelf I praife while I *his* praife intend ;
For 'tis fome virtue, virtue to commend :
And next to deeds, which our own honor raife,
Is, to diftinguifh them who merit praife.

CONGREVE.

I REALLY do not know of any inquifition of the Britifh Parliament, that is fo
little intitled to the admiration of the
Nation, as the enquiry after the Author
of this Pamphlet, and the hafty and un-
qualified cenfure of it. Our admiration
of the dignity of the legiflative and executive Powers of the State ceafes, and

our feelings, as a free people, are alarmed at the ill-timed, impolitic, and unneceffary hue and cry after a publication
that does not contain a fingle pofitive
affertion unfriendly to the eftablifhed
Government of this Country: But, on
the contrary, the ableft defence of the
true principles of Government, and a
moft mafterly expofure of the ruinous
doctrines of factious men, who are hardy
enough to publifh that *" they are boldly*
" animated at the profpect of the new, the fub-
" lime deftiny that awaits their fellow creatures."
What that NEW and SUBLIME DESTINY
is, which fo boldly animates them, we
cannot contemplate without the ftrongeft emotion and the greateft apprehenfion
for the fecurity of Government. It has,
however, received a fevere check from
this Author, who has been grofly mifreprefented for his pamphlet, which has been fo
violently cenfured and fo rafhly condemned
extrajudicially, although it is a very fenfible and temperate appeal to "the quiet
" good fenfe of the Nation," and has not
the leaft refemblance to the eccentric
doctrines

doctrines of *Paine*, who is an avowed
Enemy to our Conſtitution: The work
contains, in the paſſage that has given
moſt offence, the ſpeculative opinion of
a well-known friend to our Government,
who, it has been acknowledged by high
authority, has contributed greatly to the
ſupport of its dignity, and to the peace
and ſecurity of the Kingdom; and who,
upon this occaſion, writes theoretically,
aſſerts well-known facts, and with great
temper leaves the deduction to the public: A deduction that is not impoſed
like the ſtrong and peſtilent writings of
Paine, but which appeals ſo gently to
our underſtandings as to leave to the
clear comprehenſion and unbiaſſed judg-
ment of a well-informed, candid, and
ſpirited Nation.

The conduct of Parliament, which
ſhould always be dignified and juſt, would
in this inſtance deſerve our pity, did it
not too ſeriouſly affect the right of free-
thinking, the liberty of the preſs, and the
principles of our Conſtitution, of which

the

the Author's Accufers affect to be very
jealous, while they themfelves plunge a
dagger in its very bowels, as I fhall have
more than on one occafion to fhew.

The Parliament affumes an *inquifitorial*
capacity, in this, as it has improperly
done in other cafes, which the Houfe of
Commons, as purely legiflative, does not
poffefs. It would be abfurd in the ex-
treme, to fuppofe that the power of reprefentation, delegated by the people for
legiflative purpofes, fhould conftitute an
inquifitorial authority over them for judicial purpofes. It is perhaps the greateft
beauty of our Confttution, that neither
of the three Eftates of the Kingdom pof-
fes an inquifitorial capacity, the fecond
branch excepted, and that is a Court of
Appeal from the judicial authority : It
would be congenial with the fyftem of
an abfolute Government were either the
legiflative or executive power to poffefs
an inquifitorial jurifdiction. The idea is
a *monftrum horrendum* in a free ftate : It
is a grofs perverfion of the Legiflature,
commonly

commonly called the Conftitution; and as grofs a Libel on the judicial Authority, or the Laws of the Land: It is Treafon againft a Government that wifely keeps the authorities of the State afunder.

When the people delegate their con-ftitutional or legiflative rights, they do not inveft their Reprefentatives with any judicial authority whatever. And fince they poffefs no jurifdiction but what they receive from their conftituents, for the general purpofes of the people, from what fource do they derive an inquifitorial capacity? As they do not receive it from either the regal, or the executive, or the judicial authorities of the State, it is manifeft that it is not derived from either the Conftitution or the Law of the Land. That authority is therefore affumed by the Parliament, without de-riving it from the nature of legiflative delegation, or from the principles of the Britifh Government. It is an arbitrary affumption of power, and fuch an ufur-

pation

pation of power as plunges a dagger in the bowels of the Conſtitution.

It will perhaps be ſaid, that this inquiſitorial authority has been often exerciſed in a *high tone* by the Houſe of Commons, which I admit; but that admiſſion does not eſtabliſh their right to it. On the contrary it ſhews, to the misfortune of the Engliſh Nation, and to the reproach of their Government, how often they have perverted delegation and repreſentation by abuſing their conſtitutional authority, which is purely legiſlative, not having any inquiſitorial juriſdiction whatever over the public. Should *precedents* be againſt my opinion, I maintain that an aſſumption of power (unauthoriſed by the Conſtitution and the Law) at one period does not juſtify it at another; and that all power which is not fairly derived from either of thoſe ſources of a free State, may be juſtly and ſhould be effectually reſiſted as uſurpations dangerous to a ſyſtem of national liberty; that is, as being violent

lent and arbitrary exertions, fubverfive of our Conftitution or eftablifhed Government.

‹ The cafe of Dr. Sacheverel only tends to fhew the temper and the principles of thofe times. In our hiftory many inftances of an affumed power, incompatible with reprefentation and the rights and intereft of the people, are to be found, but what do they prove? The corruption and proftitution of the *penfioned* Parliament of Charles II. is not the only inftance of legiflative perverfion, and yet who will produce it as a precedent to juftify the principle? What is *malum in fe* cannot be juftified in equity; and what is *malum prohibitum* is not to be juftified in law.

But without going fo far back, like Mr. Sheridan, to that unabafhed reign when the Nation had a venal and proftituted Parliament, we have a recent cafe in point: A cafe that muft fill every mind with horror, and all Europe

and

and Afia with aftonifhment. The cafe
of Mr. Haftings, by which the Houfe
of Commons affumed an inquifitorial
capacity, and the Houfe of Lords a
judicial authority, difgraced the Nation,
and tended effentially to fubvert the Conftitution, under the pompous pretences
of national equity and public juftice.
But a fpecious pretence does not always
juftify the act. Defpotifm has the faireft
pretences, and tyranny the ableft advo-
cates, and yet they are the greateft of
human calamities. The whole of the
proceedings in that cafe were, in my
apprehenfion, a folemn mockery of juftice, a FARCE more ludicrous than any
thing in the works of Cervantes. The
Commons erected a Tribunal, like a
Catholic Inquifition, became informers
and accufers, and brought their random
charges before the Houfe of Lords, which
is not a Court of Juftice in the firft inftance, that is, it has no judicial authority over the people but in cafes of
appeal. As thefe proceedings were not
authorifed by any power known to the
Conftitution

Conftitution or the Laws of the Land, fo they ended as might be expected— *in fumo.*

It is not for me to fay there was not a mixture of great merit and fome blame in the Afiatic adminiftration of Mr. Haftings, as, from the imperfection of human nature, there muft neceffarily be in all adminiftrations where there is great complication of bufinefs; and particularly in a high fituation where much depended upon circumftances and upon his fuperior judgement for want of the beaten road of European Government; but I contend, that if he was amenable to any authority in Europe for mifconduct in Afia (which I very much doubt) it was to the judicial, and not to the legiflative power of his country. I am fo clearly convinced that the Conftitution and the Law have been grofly violated in this cafe, which was a truft from the Eaft India Company, highly commended by his employers, and not a truft from the Nation, or in which the

B   Nation

Nation had any concern or jurifdiction, that I do not fcruple to declare it to be my humble opinion, that Mr. Haftings has been unhappily and indeed cruelly robbed of his Peace, his Conftitution, his Character, and his Property, by a profecution totally unauthorifed and un-neceffary, and founded upon a dangerous affumption of power in the two Houfes of Parliament: An affumption that is infinitely more alarming, as being more dangerous to the Conftitution, than the fpeculative and harmlefs opinions of the Author of " Thoughts on the Englifh " Governments."

I have not made this remark fo much in juftice to Mr. Haftings, as in juftice to the Conftitution, which I think is abufed under the faireft pretences to virtue and public juftice, by affuming an inquifitorial power not congenial with legiflation: A power that I apprehend fhould never be exercifed by the legifla-tive jurifdiction, nor admitted by a free people, be the pretence what it may:

For,

For, can any thing ftrike our minds with greater horror, as a free Nation, than the idea of a legiflative Tribunal, like that of a Catholic Inquifition, hunting for witneffes, and examining them upon interrogatories to ground a criminal charge before an incompetent jurifdiction, inftead of bringing the people fairly, in all cafes whatever, before the judicial authority to which alone they are amenable for the purpofes of truth and fubftantial juftice. The moft fcrupulous advocate for the privileges of the Lords and Commons will not have the face to fay, that the judgement of Parliament is according to the Laws of the Land, which require the judgement of the peoples' *Peers,*

Returning to the Author of "Thoughts " on the Englifh Government," whofe Advocate I am proud to be, notwithftanding the hafty and ftrong condemnation of the Houfe of Commons; I contend that this arbitrary affumption of power does, under a fpecious pretence of defending the

privileges

privileges of one branch of the Conftitution, fap the foundation of the whole.
There is infinitely more danger to our
Conftitution from the affumption of an
inquifitorial capacity in that Houfe, than
in the fpeculative opinions of this or
any other Author of equal delicacy and
attachment to our Government; becaufe
the theoretical opinions of fuch enlightened men and good fubjects are perfectly
harmlefs.

The following paffage, which is confidered as the moft exceptionable, is an
illuftration of this truth: "In fine the
" Government of England is a *Monarchy*;
" the Monarchy is the ancient ftock
" from which have fprung the goodly
" branches of the Legiflature the Lords
" and Commons that, at the fame time
" give ornament to the Tree and fhelter
" to thofe who feek protection under it:
" But thefe are ftill only branches, and
" derive their origin and their nutriment
" from their common parent; they may
" be lopped off and the Tree is ftill a
" Tree;

" Tree; fhorn indeed of its honors, but
" not like them caft into the fire: The
" Kingly Government *may* go on, in all
" its functions, without Lords or Com-
" mons: It has hitherto done fo for
" years together, and in our times it
" does fo during every recefs of Parlia-
" ment."

Here the facts are felf-evident and
the conclufion incontrovertible: But, although they are both as clear as any
mathematical demonftration, they prove
nothing. Indeed theory never does: Spe-
culative opinions affert ideas that float
upon the human mind without contending for the neceffity of their adoption;
and therefore the proof of utility and
expediency is left to the conviction and
judgement of the public. *Englifhmen* have
an inherent and conftitutional right (that
is, a natural right fecured to them by
the nature of their Government) to
fpeak of the principles and effects of a
Government intirely monarchical, or an
abfolute monarchy; of the nature and
tendency

tendency of Ariftocracy; and of the principles and effects of Democracy; either feparately, or as they are connected with a monarchical fyftem, commonly called a mixed Government, or a limited monarchy.

In treating of thefe fubjects, which fo intimately concern all civilized human nature, the contemplation would be ufelefs to civilization were they not to give an opinion, and leave mankind to confider which fyftem is beft adapted to the genius and policy of their refpective States; namely, a Government intirely monarchical; a limited monarchy; or a republican Government. If Nations have made the felection, it does not preclude fpeculative opinions founded on the effects which their various fyftems have produced for the purpofe of reconfideration and comparifon. Human wifdom, which is often called public virtue, arifes from that reflection which experience occafions. Human nature is ever, by the improvement of civilization, in

fearch

fearch of wifdom for its happinefs and
fecurity. At one period this nation
thought itfelf happy under the Stuarts;
at another period that royal race was
exnelled from motives very different to
thofe which expelled the Roman Tar-
quins: That Royal fabric, founded on
the hereditary right of ages, became like
" the bafelefs fabric of a vifion." I do
not here contemplate on the wifdom
or folly of a nation, diftinguifhed for
juftice, in expelling a whole race for the
weaknefs of one prince whofe folly could
not, in reafon, or by any human laws,
incapacitate his Succeffors; but, after
fuch a Revolution in the Succeffion,
who will fay, that the fyftems of the
European Governments will preferve for
ever their prefent forms *in toto.*

It is faid that ",this Country is al-
" lowed, not only by Englifh but by the
" ableft Foreign Writers on the fubject of
" Government, to enjoy the wifeft and beft
" Syftem of Government in the known
" world." Were this national prepoffef-
fion to be admitted, does it prove the infallibility

fallibility and immutability of our fyftem?
A conftitution may be theoretically good
and practically bad. As a proof of its
fuperior wifdom we are told, that " the
" Three different Eftates of the Kingdom
" are fo conftituted and fo counterpoifed
" as to be mutual checks to each other;
" and if any one link of the chain of
" Government is to be deftroyed, by its
" being taken away, the whole Syftem
" muft be diffolved." This may be the
opinion of one man and not of another:
And I know of no Law, divine or humane,
that can oblige me to be of this opinion
if I am not convinced.

The three Eftates, or branches of our
Government, were certainly intended to
be a check on each other, and were,
therefore, fo counterpoifed as to produce
that great, that happy effect; for in that
check confifts the beauty of our Conftitution. Here I fay nothing of the depend-
ence of the fecond on the firft Eftate and
the influence of both on the third, inconfiftent with that intended check, which
is the great object of the Conftitution;
but

but if this wife *equilibrium* is deſtroyed by the Commons aſſuming an indepenent Sovereign Power in all Money Bills (the very ſoul of Legiſlation and ſupport of Government) what becomes of the mutual check ſo neceſſary to ſuch a mixed ſyſtem? If therefore that deſign is perverted; if the Commons encroach on the *equal* privilegeṣ of the other Houſe of Parliament, and render its authority paſſive in the moſt intereſting concerns of the Nation, does it prove the perfection and immutability of our Conſtitution? And if alſo the Commons, in a legiſlative juriſdiction, aſſume an inquiſitorial capacity over the people, to examine and condemn them extrajudicially, how do " we enjoy the " wifeſt and beſt ſyſtem of Government " in the world?"

It is ſaid, that " if one link of the chain " of Government is removed the whole " ſyſtem will be diſſolved." But as this is not a neceſſary conſequence ſo it is not a juſt concluſion. A link in any chain may be removed without rendering the reſt uſeleſs; nay, it may in this caſe, as in

* C   other

other inſtances, make it ſtronger: For, by removing the weak and uſeleſs parts, it will give ſolidity and permanency to the reſt. It would, at one time, have been thought Treaſon to ſuppoſe the poſſibility of an alteration in the Conſtitution or Government of Scotland; and yet time, that changes the body politic like the body natural, has totally overthrown the ſcottiſh Conſtitution by a ſtrange ſort of an Union with England, which abſorbed their Parliament and laid their indepedent Legiſlature at the feet of the Engliſh Government. I ſay ſtrange becauſe the Scots relinquiſhed their Legiſlature and preſerved their Juriſprudence: One would have thought that by being ſubject to the ſame Conſtitution they would have been governed by exactly the ſame Laws. I do not conſider the effects of this Union, whether good or bad to the ſcottiſh Nation; but I ſpeak of the event to illuſtrate my poſition that " all Conſtitutions or " forms of Government are ſubject to " change," for *what will not time produce?*

It is, therefore, the moſt prepoſterous
idea

idea in the Englifh to account it Treafon
to difpute the eternity and immutability of
their Conftitution, which I have fhewn,
in two great inftances, is perverted by the
Houfe of Commons. As well may they
pretend to the infallibility of Members of
Parliament, fome of whom would difcredit any Government. The Irifh have perhaps the fame notions as the Englifh of
the immortality of their Conftitution, and
yet it is probable that their Conftitution,
like that of Scotland, may in a few years
be abforbed by an union with Great Britain. The end of all Government (*i. e.* the
purpofe of every Conftitution) is not to
perpetuate any particular fyftem of this
or that Country, but to make it as conducive as poffible to the wifdom of the Laws
and to the happinefs of the people governed, for in their profperity confifts the
dignity of the State and the energy of
Executive Government.

And fince viciffitude is the lot of imperfect human nature, may not a free people,
who are not galled with the fetters of
defpotifm and tyranny, venture to contemplate on the effects of the various

forms

forms of Government, without "a breach
" of the privileges" of any one part of
them? I have as great veneration as any
man for the fyftem of Government which
has been adopted by my country; but,
great as my refpect is for our Conftitution, I do not think it without great
defects; not fo much from it's original
inftitution as from its abufe, arifing from
the fectarifm of a free State, and from
the force of luxury that pervades Europe
and Afia.

If at that period of our hiftory which
is fo improperly called the Revolution,
men were more than ever lavifh in their
praifes of a Government founded on
three Eftates of the Kingdom, namely,
an union of the Monarchical, Ariftocratical and Democratical parts, it was
becaufe they fuppofed the three branches
of the Conftitution would produce the
greateft happinefs to a free people, and
the greateft fecurity to liberty and property. They did not, however, expect
this Conftitution to be immutable, or
the laws founded upon it to be infallible.
Such an idea would be a libel on human
wifdom.

wifdom. Time has indeed fhewn the fuperiority of our Conftitution over the other Governments of Europe, but it has alfo difcovered its great defects, for where is perfection to be found? And as thefe defects are of great magnitude, can it be wondered that ingenious men fhould give an opinion how they may be removed, and the fyftem of Government made more perfect, and, by confequence, more conducive to the dignity of the State and to the happinefs of the people? And would it not be degrading to human nature and a libel on national liberty to maintain, that the exercife of our underftandings on the principles and effects of Government, noways injurious to the Conftitution and the Laws, is a breach of the privilege of any one branch of the Legiflature? Such a charge, on fo flight a ground, is not only the affumption of an unconftitutional authority in breach of the rights of the people, but it is treating a free people like a Nation of SLAVES.

c

I fhould

I fhould be glad to know what privileges the reprefentatives of the people
poffefs over the underftanding of their
Conftituents, that when we know the
nature of them we may judge how they
have been violated, and whether it was
done intentionally or undefignedly, from
an ignorance of this *divine right* of the
Houfe of Commons. This legiflative
bugbear, which is often held out *in ter-
rorem* to the people, under the hideous
form of privileges undefined and incom-
prehenfible (the defcription of difcretionary and omnipotent power) puts me in
mind of the Catholic carpenter, who was
required to worfhip the wooden image he
had made: The carpenter knew what
he had made, as the people know what
they have created; and as the one had
too much fenfe to worfhip the work of
his own hands, fo the other will have
too much fpirit to fubmit to the oppreffion of an authority of their own
creating.

I have fhewn that fpeculative opinions

nions on the Governments of Europe, even though they fhould glance at the defects of our own and fuggeft an *alteration*, is a manner of writing confiftent with the liberty of the prefs, and with the inherent and conftitutional rights of Englifhmen: I have alfo laughed at the humiliating Idea of the Parliament in charging a Writer with a Libel on their undefined privileges, for exercifing a right which ought not to be denied to the Subjects of arbitrary Governments. In the prefent cafe, which is perfectly harmlefs, unawed by the Author's high-founding parliamentary Enemies, who prove nothing but the inconfiftency of their principles and the ftrength of their paffions, I am proud to be of his opinion; but, like that able Writer and good Subject, I fubmit it with the moft becoming refpect, as all Writers on our fyftem of Government ought to do, to the fuperior, the liberal, and unerring judgement of the nation.

If my Author has alluded to any *al-*

teration

eration in our Conftitution, which confifts of three branches, as an opinion
of his own, he has the example of the
brighteft Men in the Kingdom who
have at various periods boldly contended
for a *Reform.* Does not that alteration
fo ftrongly infifted upon in both Houfes
of Parliament (which like the efforts of
Sampfon, endangers the whole fabric)
come more within the defcription of a
Libel on the Conftitution, than the modeft allufion of this Writer?

By explaining my own meaning, I
wifh to defend the fenfible Author of
" Thoughts on the Englifh Govern-
" ment" from the treachery of fome
men, and the folly of others, who have
unmercifully attacked an harmlefs man
that fpeaks with diffidence what has
ever been the opinion, and will ever be
the wifh of Government. There is,
and I affirm it without fear of contradiction, not a fingle member of the prefent Cabinet who is not of the Author's
opinion, whatever he may affect to the
contrary.

contrary. Had I ten thoufand pounds, I would ftake the whole that it is the opinion *una voce* and the wifh *exanimo* of the prefent Miniftry, and indeed of every Adminiftration.

The moft exceptionable paffage, which fays that " the Government *may* go on " without Lords or Commons" is a truth not to be difputed; but how far that truth is confiftent with our monarchical ——ariftocratical——democratical Government the Author has not fhewn. We are therefore not to confider a tranfient paffage, which will admit of a fchifm, but the context of the pamphlet which is the fineft panegyric on good order and fubordination; the happieft defence of Executive Government at this period of feditious quixotifm; and the ableft refutation of the poifonous doctrines of Sectaries. As to the truth of the obfervation, let me afk whether Executive Government has not more energy and a better effect without the controul of Parliament? This truth alone ought to

filence

filence the Gentlemen in adminiftration and make them quite afhamed of their proceedings againft the unoffending Author, who, I contend, is ftrictly within the principles of the Conftitution, and both the letter and the fpirit of the Law, and who has a clear right to advance a fpeculative opinion, which does no more harm to this Government than it does to that of the Emperor of Morocco,

This inherent right of an Englifhman is as clear as that of his Majefty (God blefs and long preferve him) to the prerogatives of the Crown. It is therefore treafon againft a free ftate to fay that the exercife of this right is "an high breach of the privileges of the people's " Reprefentatives." Should it be afked, who will difpute the wifdom of the Houfe of Commons, that, like the judgement of God, have pronounced fuch a fentence *extrajudicially?* I anfwer; thofe who know that the Members of that Houfe are no more infallible than other men;

and

and who know alfo that they poffefs no
privileges but what are neceffary to the
purpofes of Legiflation. For my part, I
admire the modefty as much as I do the
truth of the Author. He is manifeftly
under the influence of truth alone. He
is ,no party writer: Neither the Slave
of Power or the Tool of Faction. In his
beautiful allegory, by which he happily
compares our Conftitution to a Tree,
he fays nothing invidioufly of the *rotten*
branches: He fays, and he fays truly,
that a Tree difencumbered of its *ufelefs*
branches, will retain and increafe its
vigor and its beauty!!! But, although
the truth in this comparifon is not to be
controverted, the effect on our Conftitution is like that of a pop-gun, perfectly harmlefs to our invulnerable Government. It has however produced a
Miracle. It has brought together the
two oppofite parties whofe opinions of
the Conftitution are as different as the
Poles are oppofite. There are no two
things in nature fo contrary as the opinions of thefe two parties on the Conftitution

tution of this Country, and yet they affect to agree in the prefent cafe!!! As one of the many proofs of their oppofite ideas of the Conftitution, take the following extraordinary inftance, which will fhew the folly of their agreeing even in this cafe: The one party, faithful to a great public truft, contends that " meafures, as ftrong as the occafion re-" quires, are neceffary to preferve the " authorities of the State and the happy " effects of the Conftitution;" while the other party maintain a folecifm that " the means of prevention and prefer-" vation are conducive to its fubvertion: " And that the purity of the Conftitu-" tion cannot be better preferved than " by roufing the people *en maffe*, and arm-" ing their paffions againft Govern-" ment."!!! Thus are the heterogeneous principles of avowed Enemies in unifon! And thus are the public deluded by pompous proceedings and problematical public virtue.

To return, with the indignant feelings

ings of an Englifhman from this digref-
fion: Parliaments may be neceffary to
grant the fupplies, and when they are
granted every thing elfe follows of courfe
as naturally as the effect follows the
caufe. Whatever are the true defigns
of Parliaments (with which my Com-
patriots are too well acquainted for me
to explain) their effects are a mere concurrence with the views and meafures
of Executive Government, which would
have more energy, and, in my confci-
ence I believe, a better effect without
them. I do not know whether "the
" Author of Thoughts on the Englifh
" Government" means as much as I
have expreffed; but thefe are facts not
to be controverted either by the chicane of Lawyers or the fophiftry of
Statefmen: And if they bring in queftion the *wifdom* of the Conftitution or
the *virtue* of Parliament, the Writer can
only be criminated upon the horrid
principle of a Scottifh Lawyer, that
" Truth is a Libel as well as Falfehood,

" and

" and the greater crime for being a
" Truth."

That Parliaments are the mere *echo*
of Executive Government, witnefs the
great majority of the prefent Miniftry:
And that, after the fupplies are granted,
Government could very well difpenfe
with them, witnefs the two Bills which
have convulfed the Nation. Without
that oppofition, would not the energy
and effect of Government be greater?
This will ever be tacitly admitted by
every Adminiftration. Upon what principle then can the Miniftry affift their
worft political Enemies to facrifice an
Author of acknowleged merit, who fays
no more than they think and wifh themfelves, nor I believe half fo much. To
that oppofition we may, without breach
of charity, afcribe all the evils of the
prefent day. To Members of that very
Parliament which fhould preferve the
Conftitution, as the moft facred truft,
we owe a political contagion that, like
the peftilence of the body natural, endangers

dangers its exiftence. I am not a public Incendiary, nor the Affaffin of the
Rights of the People. I fpeak of facts
which at this moment endanger the Government and threaten the total fubverfion of our Conftitution. Influenced
by truth alone, I have the courage to
charge thofe facts to Members of the
very Parliament which fhould prevent
them; and who modeftly complain of
a little breach of their *imaginary* privileges, while they are making a greater
breach in the Conftitution.

The Duke of Bedford and his Com-
peers, and Mr. Fox and his Partizans,
Members of the two Houfes of Parliament, have boldly convened the great
body of the people to affert rights they
do not poffefs, and to maintain principles
which are both repugnant to, and fubverfive of the Conftitution: They have
roufed the great mafs of the people, and
have armed the paffions of the multitude
againft the Government, and by fo rafh

a ftep

a ſtep they have plunged a dagger in the very bowels of the Conſtitution.

To ſhew the error and danger of ſuch a deluſive conduct, I maintain, that the collective body of this free ſtate have no political exiſtence whatever. By our form of Government, which is commonly called the Conſtitution, the public or community tacitly ſurrender, and as effectually as if it was done formally, their political rights in the Legiſlature to the conſtituent body, and they, to the repreſentative body, not for the purpoſes of their Conſtituents in particular, but of the Nation at large. Hence ariſes univerſal and equal repreſentation, as effectually as if every member of the community had a vote at the conſtitutional period of electing their Repreſentatives, without the miſchief of univerſal ſuffrage, ſo ſtrongly and ſo erroneouſly contended for by the Duke of Richmond.

The people have an undoubted right to petition againſt grievances or meaſures, which

which they conceive to be fubverfive of their privileges and intereft; but the nature of that right fhould be underftood. Upon this important fubject Lord Thurlow ftated "the undoubted right of the "people to petition the King, or either "Houfe of Parliament, upon any real or "fuppofed grievance; and that was a "liberty which he trufted would remain "intire and unfhaken by any reftraint "whatever." But that high authority does not explain the nature of that right nor what is meant by the people: The learned Lord is too well acquainted with our Government to fay it means the Populace or the Nation at large, whofe rights are wifely abforbed by a compreffion into a fmaller compafs. As the right of election is exclufively in the conftituent part of the public, for the purpofes of the whole, fo is the right of petitioning confined to that body. And fince the rights of the collective body are clearly and totally abforbed by the conftituent power, fo the *vox populi*, or the voice of the populace, can only be heard

by

by the Reprefentatives of the people, through the only conftitutional channel, namely, the organ of their Conftituents. To talk of the rights of the people in general to affemble and petition the Legiflature for fuppofed grievances, is talking like a madman; or, what is worfe, like a public incendiary, who roufes the multitude, and arms their paffions againft the Peace and Government of the Nation.

Party-men are continually telling the Public that they have a right to petition the Parliament, in certain cafes that greatly affect them, and *fo they have*; but unlefs they tell them the nature of their right, that it is confined to the conftituent part of the Nation, they may, as in the prefent inftance, be led into fuch an error as endangers the public peace and the fecurity of Government. The BILL of RIGHTS, which is a Bill *explanatory* of the rights of the people, means the rights derived from the nature of a free Government, and are confined to the conftituent body

body for the purpofes of the whole; and not the right of every individual to petition either the Throne or the Parliament, which would be attended with endlefs confufion, fubverfive of the tranquillity of the Nation, and the great ends of Government. The collecting of names to Party-Petitions, proves nothing in their favor, however numerous and refpectable they may be for rank and property, unlefs they are from the conftituent body of the people, regularly convened and conftitutionally exercifing their exclufive right to be heard by their Reprefentatives. All other petitions, offered to the two Houfes of Parliament, fhould be rejected as affuming a right which the Petitioners do not poffefs, incompatible with the exclufive right of the conftituent body and the dignity of Parliament. The individual petition of Major Cartwright was a proof either of great ignorance of the Conftitution, or great prefumption, peculiar to the arrogance of party; and the admiffion of that Petition was as great an error in the Houfe of Commons. The

The Duke of Bedford prefented one to the Houfe of Lords figned by 13,793 perfons, inhabitants of London and its environs, agreed to at a Meeting near Copenhagen-houfe, Iflington, in the County of Middlefex. The very defcription of the perfons and the place of meeting, muft fhew the impropriety of admitting the petition, which is a Libel on the Conftitution, and on the virtue and wifdom of the Ariftocratic part of our Government. The Conftituent part of the Nation in their *refpective diftricts* of London, Weftminfter and Middlefex, to which the inhabitants belong, have a right to petition, but not the populace. If therefore the noble Duke, as a young Statesman, is not fufficiently acquainted with the vaft difference between the conftituent and the collective part of the people, if he does not know *where* they fhould meet, and *how* they fhould petition the two branches of the Legiflature called the Parliament, the noble Houfe, with fo much experience, fhould fhew its wifdom and regard to the true principles

ciples of the Conftitution, by rejecting
all petitions which have not a conftitutional right to be heard; fince the receiving of any other, in breach of the
exclufive right of the conftituent part
of the public to be heard by petition, is
an infult offered to the wifdom and dignity of the fecond branch of the Legiflature. His Grace of Bedford, as a young
politician, may be fomewhat excufable
for not poffeffing a perfect knowledge of
the true principles of our Government;
but Mr. Fox, who is a veteran in politics,
is unpardonable for being guilty of Treafon againft the Conftitution; for fuch
muft be the crime of any man, be his
rank what it may, who can roufe the
great mafs of the people againft the neceffary meafures of Government, without
any real caufe, or any conftitutional right
for their refiftance. The Right Hon.
Gentleman affects to preferve the deareft
rights of the people while he takes the
moft effectual means to deftroy them and
the public peace, by fapping the foundation of the conftitution, and bringing the

E   noble

noble edifice of legiſlative and executive
authority to the ground.

This is a ſtrong inſtance in point : It
ſhews that the energy and effect of Executive Government would be greater
without the *oppoſition* of Parliament, in
which there is at preſent ſtrong ſeeds
of contagion and diſſolution truly alarming to the Conſtitution; and for which
there ſeems to be only one remedy,
namely, a *reſolute* Government, unſhaken
by the dangerous principles of falſe friends,
and determined (with the bleſſings of
heaven upon the beſt intentions and the
ableſt endeavors) to cure the wounds
given to the body politic, and the alarming danger to the public ſecurity ariſing
from the daring attempts of reſtleſs and
deſigning men, who wiſh to overthrow
the Government and diſſolve the Conſtitution.

This inſtance, which impeaches the
virtue and infallibility of Parliament,
pleads forcibly in favor of the Author of
“ Thoughts

" Thoughts on the Englifh Government:"
It fhews that if his allegory throws a
flight reflection, which probably was never meant, on two branches of the Legiflature, inconfiftent with the dignity
of Parliament, it is but a tranfient glance,
and perfectly harmlefs when compared
with the greater indignity offered by
Members of the two Houfes to the Conftitution, by advifing the great body of
the people to affemble and affert rights
they do not poffefs; and the ftill greater
indignity to the Nation, by affuming
an inquifitorial capacity, and pronounc-
ing a criminal fentence, contrary to the
principles of the judicial authority, and
in breach of the exclufive privileges of
that jurifdiction.

Should the Author be found guilty
after this *extrajudicial* fentence, by a *com-*
petent authority, of a " Libel on the pri-
" vileges of Parliament," the fame authority that is competent to his conviction
cannot avoid, from principles of fubftantial and impartial juftice, finding a part

of

of the two Houfes of Parliament guilty of a more " malicious, fcandalous, and " feditious Libel, tending to create jealou- " fies and divifions among His Majefty's " fubjects, to alienate their affections " from our happy Government, to fub- " vert the true principles of our free " Conftitution," by roufing the great mafs of the people, and arming them with unconftitutional and alarming re- fiftance to the neceffary meafures of the Legiflature.

I do not fay, neither does the Au- thor of " Thoughts on the Englifh Go- " vernment," that the branches which are either corrupt or ufelefs *fhould* be lopped off; but I maintain that we have a right to fay they *might* be lopped off without impairing the Conftitution; nay, I may go further and fay the event would, in *my apprehenfion*, give life and vigour and energy to the Conftitu- tion of the body politic. Right or wrong as the idea may be, I contend that, as the fubject of a free ftate, I

have

have a right to the opinion, and that
there exifts no conftitutional or legal
power whatever to deprive me of its
utterance. The fenfible and *cautious* Author of the above pamphlet advances
a fpeculative opinion and leaves it to
the judgement of the Public to accept
or rejeÆt it as it may ftrike their minds:
But were one half of the Nation to
think exaÆtly as he does in that ref-
peÆt, it would not prove any thing
to the injury of the Conftitution; and
where there is no injury intended or
effeÆted there can be no crime for the
cognizance of any authority whatever.

Is there a man of letters in the
Kingdom that will difpute the faÆts as
flightly ftated by the Author? Is there
any criminality or culpability in ftating
faÆts which are as manifeft as any mathematical demonftration? But it will
perhaps be faid that if there is no harm
in relating hiftorical faÆts there is mifchief in drawing conclufions dangerous
to the exifting *forms* of Government.

In

In fome cafes it may be true, but not
in the prefent inftance; fince what the
Author fays is as harmlefs as it is true.
Indeed the Writer of the pamphlet intitled, "Thoughts on the Englifh Go-
" vernment" could never think of making an unfavorable and lafting impref-
fion by the paffage which has given
offence, for he but *gently fkims upon the
furface.*

But were he fuppofed to be guilty
of any crime againft either of the three
branches of the Conftitution, he is fubject to the Laws of his Country and
amenable only to the judicial Authority.
The unauthorifed conduct of the Houfe
of Commons in this cafe is truly alarming. It erects itfelf into an Inquifition
and pronounces judgement in its own
caufe, contrary to the principles and
practice of every Court of juftice. It
ufurps the power of the judicial jurifdiction and offers a much greater indignity to the privileges of that authority
than the Author has done to the privileges

leges of Parliament: fo that while they, in a proud imperious ftyle, cenfure and condemn by means of informers. and extorted interrogatories (the very bane of a free ftate) and prepare to profecute an ufeful Individual for a fmall fault, they commit a much greater one themfelves againft the principles of the Couftitution and the authority of the Law. *He* exercifes the right of an Englifhman to advance a fpeculative opinion the moft harmlefs, while the Parliament by which he is accufed, ufurp a dangerous power and in the true fpirit of ufurpers pronounce judgement in their own caufe. They condemn the accufed, unheard by Council, and fend their condemnation to the other Houfe of Parliament which is equally concerned in the charge for confirmation and punifhment *!!! Are thefe the admired principles of our boafted Conftitution, fuperior to all other Governments in Europe, or are they the rafh and violent principles of ufurpation and error?

* It was then intended to be brought finally before the Houfe of Lords.

If

If Minifters could, for a moment, be influenced by the trafh which their Informer has publifhed, they would deferve to be pitied as much as he is defpifed for his treachery, fervility and ignorance. *Miles* difcovers the principles of a Parafite. It would be doing too much honor to the nonfenfe of fuch a fycophant to take any notice of it. The abilities and principles of the Author of " Thoughts on the Englifh Government" will be refpected when fuch a man is totally forgotten. If the talents and public merit of thefe men were compared, how great the inequality!

> "———How much alafs,
> " One man another does furpafs"!

The three letters publifhed with the fignature of *William Miles* to Mr. Pitt and Mr. Reeves prove him to be capable of all the treachery and fervility of a political Pander. The betraying of private con-

fidence

fidence is thus beautifully defcribed by
the Poet:

> So gentle Truth does her fair Breaft difarm,
> And gives to Treachery a Power to harm.

" Such doctrines," (fays he) " as are ad-
" vanced in this pamphlet have a direct
" tendency to mifchief, to alienate the
" affections of the people from His Ma-
" jefty and his Government." This is
the rafh affertion of an ignorant fycophant, fince there is not a word in the
whole work that has the leaft defign
or the flighteft tendency to produce that
effect: nor is there a libellous expreffion
againft His Majefty or his Government
to be found in the whole production;
but, on the contrary, the true principles of fubordination, and the true means
of promoting the dignity of authority,
and the happinefs of the people.

This Informer has the impudence
and folly to fay, that " if Minifters dif-
" charge their duty they muft difcourage

F   " the

" the publication in queftion." Were they to take his advice it would not prevent its fpreading: Being condemned by authority it would be the more fought after. This is already the cafe, for a pamphlet which fold at two fhillings has fince been fold at five fhillings from the interpofition of Parliament. Nor did ever any Government that practifed impolitic feverity get any thing by it but infamy to itfelf, and renown to thofe who fuffered under it.

I am therefore of a different opinion, for two reafons, namely: One, be-caufe in a defign highly flattering to the true principles of the Conftitution in Church and State, and manifeftly conducive to the public peace and the fecurity of property by the overthrow of fedition, there does not appear to me to be any thing in the whole pro-duction offenfive to Government on which to ground their interpofition; the other becaufe the time employed, at this critical period, in perfecuting an
unoffending

unoffending Individual would be better
employed againſt thoſe great Offenders in
both Houſes of Parliament, who preach
Treaſon and invite Rebellion, by in-
veſting the great maſs of the people
with an unconſtitutional right of aſſem-
bling to endanger Executive Government, and ſubvert the conſtitutional Authorities of the State.

Parliamentary offenders have manifeſtly, and to the reproach of Government, been guilty of *more* than "a ſe-
"ditious and ſcandalous Libel, tending
"to create jealouſies and diviſions among
"His Majeſty's Subjects, to alienate their
"affections from our happy form of Go-
"vernment, and to ſubvert the true
"principles of our free Conſtitution:"
Their conduct, in miſguiding the people, and inviting their reſiſtance to the
moſt neceſſary meaſures of Government
for the public ſecurity, being not only
a high breach of the excluſive privileges
of the conſtituent power of the people,

but

but an act of Treafon againft the Conftitution.

How very ftrange muft it appear to
the admirers of the Englifh Government,
to find that the Parliament is eager to
cenfure and punifh *extrajudicially*, an Author for an harmlefs opinion, while fome
of their own Members in both Houfes,
maintain opinions the moft injurious to
the Conftitution, and the moft dangerous to Executive Government with im-
punity: Opinions which, at this moment,
endanger the public peace, and may be
attended with the moft melancholy confequences. In my apprehenfion, Executive Government acts pufilanimoufly in
both cafes: Pufilanimoufly in purfuing
an harmlefs individual, who has been,
by their own confeffion, remarkably ufeful to them and to the Nation; and
pufilanimoufly, in not purfuing the
greater enemies of good order and neceffary Government. In the latter more
than in the former cafe. " Minifters,
" if they do their duty, will difcourage
" the

" the diforder," which is as dangerous
to the body politic, as peftilence is to
the body natural. In that cafe the conduct of oppofition is, as I have obferved,
more than " a Libel, tending to create
" jealoufies and divifions among . His
" Majefty's fubjects," it is treafon, tending to fubvert the true principles of our
Conftitution or eftablifhed Government.

In the opinion of the late Earl of
Chatham, " it fhould be the pride of an
" Englifhman to think that the Con-
" ftitution of his Country can never die."
I, as an Englifhman, fincerely wifh that
its principles may have immenfity for their
fpace, and eternity for their duration.
But, notwithftanding the fincerity of my
devotion, and my ardent wifh that the
Conftitution may be immortal, I do not
think that human wifdom is infallible, or
human inftitutions immutable. It would
be an indignity to the human mind, nay,
it would be an impiety to think fo. The
Conftitution is no more immutable, than
the Laws of the Land are infallible; and
                                                  the

the fame reafons that are affigned for the improvement of the one, may be adduced for the greater perfection of the other.

When the wifdom of ancient and modern nations fixed on a fyftem of Government, they did not engage for its immutability. Every period has been fenfible of the uncertainty even of the wifeft human eftablifhments. Hence the alterations and revolutions in Government! As Nations grow enlightened by experience and reflection, they will adapt their Conftitutions and their Laws to the wifdom of the age in which they live. No man will contend that our Laws, which are either abrogated, or in fome fhape or other altered every feffion, are infallible: Nor will any man in his fenfes contend, that our Conftitution, excellent as it may be, is immutable. The prefent fyftem of limited Monarchy divided into three branches, concurring in public meafures, I fhall admire fo long as it is not abufed; . but whenever, as in the prefent and many other inftances, either

of

of the component parts, ufurp an authority, and exercife it incompatible with their fhare of the Conftitution, by converting a legiflative into a judicial authority, in breach of the rights of the people, which are of more confequence than the affumed privileges of their Reprefentatives, then I fhall not do homage to that ufurpation. Convinced thåt a Government defcribed as King, Lords and Commons, is as fubject as any other to viciffitude; I fhall think like an Englifhman, and fhall contend that experience teaches the neceffity of fupplying the imperfections of the Conftitution, as well as the inefficiency of the Law: And the cure of thefe defects in our Government, is, I believe, all that is meant by the modeft Author of " Thoughts on " the Englifh Government," who has not faid a fingle word againft the omnipotence of Parliament, but only fays, that the unneceffary branches of a tree may be lopped off without any injury to the trunk.

He

He is indeed accufed by Party-men, who feel extremely fore of maintaining, that, AN INDEPENDENT HOUSE OF COMMONS IS NO PART OF THE ENGLISH CONSTITUTION" though not a fingle word of that quotation is to be found in the pamplet. *Stage trick* may have the intended effect, but this trick of party, to impofe on a candid and liberal Public, offers an infult to the underftanding and juftice of that part of the Nation who have read the publication, and who will find that, although the well-informed and temperate Author has happily expofed the folly of men who talk fo much about the Conftitution and the Revolution, he has faid very little about the Parliament. Mr. Sheridan is not more unfortunate in this mifquotation, and his mifreprefentation of the Author, in this inftance, than in the precedent he found in the reign of Charles II. Does he mean to compare the profligacy of that reign with the virtue of the prefent? Or does he mean to compare the treacherous conduct of the penfioned and proftituted

tuted Parliament of that unabaſhed period, to the difintereſted wifdom of the
preſent Parliament ? ! ! !

If he wiſhes for a precedent in this
caſe, he ſhould look for one ſubſequent
to the period called the Revolution, a
period which ſhould bury in oblivion all
acts of injuſtice and oppreſſion. That
period ſhould be confidered rather as a
Renovation of our Government, than a
Revolution in it, for my Author has ably
and clearly ſhewn it was no Revolution
at all. A Revolution is occaſioned either
by foreign conqueſt, or domeſtic ſubver-
ſion of the former ſyſtem of Government,
neither of which happened at that period. The emancipation of North America, and the overthrow of the monarchical Government in France, were
Revolutions, but I contend that the
Engliſh had no Revolution in 1688, nor
any thing like a Revolution: Since they
had the very ſame monarchical Government at, and ſubſequent to that period,
as before it.

G

If

If the Englifh Nation fent for a Dutch Prince, and placed him upon the Throne inftead of the Royal Houfe of Stuart, and if they thought proper to expel the ancient and hereditary Princes of that illuftrious Houfe, and call it the abdication of James II. which went to the expulfion of the whole race for the weaknefs or folly of one Prince, did that exchange of their own Princes for a Dutch Officer,* without any alteration in their Government, occafion a Revolution, which implies a total fubverfion of Government, like thofe great events in America and France?

As a proof that the year 1688 produced no Revolution in this country, let me afk any Englifhman whether the people did at that period *revolt*, as in the above inftances; or whether they exchanged or in any manner altered their

---

* The Stadtholder called the Prince of Orange, as Captain, General, &c. is the firft Civil and Military officer of the Batavian Republic.

fyftem

fyftem of Government? Was not their Conftitution or eftablifhed forms of Government the fame before as fubfequent to that period? The Bill of Rights was indeed, like the Revolution, fuppofed to be an acquifition, but it was, in reality, none. It was nothing more than a Bill *declaratory* of the peoples' rights: It was no conceffion whatever; but an acknowledgement of what they were *ever* intitled to, from the nature of a Monarchy limited by Laws. The idea therefore, of " fupporting the CONSTI-" TUTION according to the principles of " the GLORIOUS REVOLUTION of 1688," is a palpable abfurdity in fo great a Lawyer as Mr. Erfkine; fince we had abfolutely no Revolution at that period, nor were any new principles eftablifhed at that time.

If it is folly to call this event in 1688 a Revolution, which had abfolutely nothing of the nature or effects of a Revolution in it; it is equally abfurd to fpeak fo much of the glorious memory

G 2

of our great deliverer King William,
That Prince did no more than was natural to preferve the Crown which had
been given to him either by the caprice
or generofity of the Englifh Nation. He
is ftiled our great deliverer, but I am at
a lofs to conceive from what danger he
delivered this country? My Author is
therefore perfectly right in affigning to
thefe events their true motives, and de-
fcribing them by their true names. In
doing this he acts like a faithful Hiftorian, and for the truth he modeftly
appeals not to the paffions and prejudices of party, but to " the quiet GOOD
" SENSE of an enlightened Nation."
Eminently diftinguifhed for candor and
liberality.

Here I defire leave, in imitation of
this fenfible and well-difpofed Author,
to obferve that if the Englifh Nation
wifh for a memorable period, equal to
any that foreign States can boaft of,
inftead of imaginary Revolution let them
felicitate themfelves on the Honoverian
Succeffion,

Succeffion. That indeed was a great,
a glorious event; fince it will be acknowledged, with pride and national
gratitude, that the Princes of that illuftrious Houfe have underftood the
principles of civil and religious liberty,
better than any that have fat upon
the Throne of this Kingdom. From
that *æra* the Englifh fhould date the
fecurity of their liberty and property.
It fhould therefore be commemorated
as the moft glorious event; which, with
the bleffings of Providence upon the
Brunfwick race, will have immenfity for
its fpace and eternity for its duration.
That event has been truly glorious.
At no period of our Hiftory have we
feen the Sovereign Power give fuch
proofs of attachment to the true principles of our Government as fince the
Hanoverian Succeffion. The virtues of
the amiable Monarch now on the throne
deferve immortality: His Majefty will
be claffed, by the faithful Hiftorian,
with the immortal Roman who was
both the admiration of his own Empire

and

and *the delight of Mankind.* Let us then forget the folly of an imaginary Revolution and commemorate with raptures the glorious Succeffion of the Houfe of Brunfwick, which has realized and fecured the true principles of civil Liberty.

Thefe great truths upon Record lead me to my Author's ideas of a monarchical Government, which are too loofe to merit the exception taken to them. Although the Parliament affect to be very tenacious of their privileges, it is evident, from our Hiftory, that the Commons have incroached greatly on the prerogatives of the Crown and the privileges of the Peers. "As foon as "the Lords and Commons met" (fays Rapin) "in two different Houfes or dif-"tinct Chambers, the Commons look-"ed on themfelves as the *fole* genuine "Reprefentatives of the people by whom "they were chofen; and in procefs of "time were confidered as Guardians of "the principles, liberties, and depofitaries "of the Kingdom. Hence the Commons,

"as

" as Reprefentatives of the people, claim
" an inconteftible right of laying taxes and
" granting money to the King, in which
· " cafe the Lords have no other power
" than barely acceding to the bill in
" queftion or rejecting it without altera-
" tion or amendment. And fo tenacious
" are the Commons of this exclufive
" right that they would reject any money
" bill that was in the leaft altered by
" the Houfe of Lords."

Hence it is manifeft that our Government or Conftitution has ever been monarchical except when it was fubverted by
Cromwell; and that Parliaments were
nothing more than appendages of a
Monarchy, limited by law, which are
fufpended *durante bene placito* of the Sovereign, who having the fupreme power
of calling and diffolving them, many in
my apprehenfion, totally difpenfe with
them without any injury to the Conftitution or good Government of this Country. This is my opinion, other perfons
have a right to think otherwife according

ing to their conviction. I do not wish to make Converts, but I claim a right to think according to the conviction of my own mind.

Why the Commons confider themfelves as the *fole* Guardians of the people and the Depofitaries of the Kingdom, I cannot conceive, confiftent with the equal fhare of the other Houfe of Parliament; nor upon what principle of Legiflation they can claim an exclufive right to Money Bills unaltered, becaufe they originate with them, is beyond my comprehenfion. It is a folecifm in the Legiflation of a Free State incompatible with the equal rights of the two Branches of the Conftitution, called the Parliament, to promote the dignity of the Crown and the intereft of the people.

The Houfe of Commons have always had high notions of their privileges, and although they are all derived from the people and exercifed in their name, and for their purpofes, they have, in many
inftances,

inftances, pretended that the people had violated their delegated privileges by difputing their omnipotence. Thus the power delegated affumes an authority over their Conftituents and become a fort of Sovereign Subjects! This is a folecifm in our Government arifing from the pufillanimity of the Public in fubmitting to the affumed inquifitorial capacity of their Reprefentatives in the Legiflature.

Upon the whole, the Conftitution of Parliaments, like other Conftitutions, has its good and its bad qualities, its ufes and its imperfections. Its good qualities are its *legiflative* attention to the true intereft of the State and to the true ends of a monarchical Government; its imperfections are its inquifitorial capacity, by which they ufurp a power over the people which was never delegated to them, and which is incompatible with delegation and reprefentation, and a breach of the exclufive right of the judicial authority of the Nation. Thefe incroach-

H   ments,

ments, under pretence of preserving
imaginary privileges, may one day roufe
the people to throw off the yoke of oppreffion; and when they are emanci-
pated from the fetters of the very power
which they have created and which exifts folely from their authority and for
their purpofes, it will perhaps be confidered how far Parliaments are neceffary
to a monarchical Government?

In the prefent cafe the very proceedings of the two Houfes of Parliament
juftify a reflection on the utility of them:
They get entirely out of their own jurifdiction—they ufurp another for the purpofe of coercion—they arbitrarily fend
for whom they pleafe, to examine them
upon interrogatories, like a Catholic Inquifition—they feize a man's papers and
imperioufly charge his own fervants to
give evidence and produce his own papers
againft him. And this glaring ufurpation
of authority and violation of every principle of jurifprudence and juftice, is under color of defending the *imaginary* privileges.

vileges of two branches of the Legiſlature, which I contend the Author of
" Thoughts on the Engliſh Government"
has not half ſo much injured as they
have in the preſent Seſſion injured the
excluſive right of the conſtituent part
of the public, and, by conſequence, the
principles of the Conſtitution.

Were I capable of adviſing Miniſters,
it ſhould be to turn their miſtaken and
miſapplied vengeance againſt that unoffending Author, and defend the ſa-
cred principles of the Conſtitution which
have been violently attacked by Members of Parliament. The vengeance of
the Law ſhould fall on thoſe who endanger the Government by the worſt
principles and the moſt alarming attempts
to ſubvert it:

"――――For juſtice bears the arm of God,
" And the graſp'd Vengeance only waits his Nod."

CAWTII.

It is a melancholy proof either of the

H 2   imper-

imperfection or abufe of our Conftitution, that Members of the two Houfes
of Parliament can be fo folicitous to
purfue and punifh the Author of
" Thoughts on the Englifh Government,"
while they are, at the fame time, infinitely more criminal by roufing the multitude and arming them with miftaken
rights and ftrong prejudices againft the
moft neceffary meafures of Government,
taken for the peace and fecurity of the
Nation. Should he be rafhly punifhed,
and they efcape a legal punifhment, it
will put me in mind of the farcaftic obfervation of Sir Samuel Garth:

"Little Villains muft fubmit to Fate,
"While greater Rogues enjoy the world in State."

The defence of this Author's pamphlet,
which I very much admire, gives me a
fine opportunity to bring a more ferious
charge againft his Accufers, who affect
to be jealous of a Sprig of the Conftitution while they lay the axe to the
Trunk.

Many

Many·are the inftances in which the
Houfe of Commons have affumed an
high toned inquifitorial capacity, and
claimed the right of the Civil Power to
commit, and of the Judicial Power to examine witneffes and pronounce judgement
on thofe who have incurred their difpleafure. I cannot think the framers of
our Government meant this tyranny!
No: The Parliament ufurp an authority
which the Conftitution never intended
they fhould take. In every inftance
therefore, that has come to my knowledge, I have advifed difobedience to an
affumed authority that violates our Law
and abufes our Conftitution. I have
great refpect for the component parts of
our Legiflature, but I refpect them in
the exercife of their functions and not in
the abufe of them. Whenever the people are fuppofed to offend they are ame-
able to the Laws of their Country and
not to any one branch of the Legiflature,
not even to the King who is the fupreme
part of the Conftitution and the Law,
being at the head of the Church and State.
The

The inquifitorial authority exercifed by the Privy Council, or Executive Power, and by the Houfe of Commons, as a legiflative Power, are grofs violations of the Conftitution and encroachments upon the privileges of the people. The cafe of Mr. Haftings was a pompous nothing: It was a Libel on the juftice of this Country, and Treafon againft the Law: For under color of juftice *from the Laws of this Nation* the Legiflature ufurped the jurifdiction of the judicial authority, the only power to which Englifhmen are fubject.

Another recent inftance muft fill every mind with horror and every breaft with indignation: I mean the abominable report of the Secret Committee to prejudice the minds of the Public at large, and the Jury in particular, who were to fit in judgement with minds totally unbiaffed againft men *illegally* apprehended upon a *fictious* charge of Treafon. Thefe proceedings were atrocious and abominable; they were a grofs perverfion of our mild Laws and a grofs Libel on our

boafted

boaſted Conſtitution, or the reputed mild and liberal Government of this Country. I do not mean to be an Advocate for men, who, under the moſt alarming circumſtances of the Na tion from foreign War and domeſtic Commotion, were charged with ſeditious practices to increaſe the ferment and endanger Government; but I wiſh to mark with ſtrong reprobation, the high toned conduct of the Houſe of Commons, in exerciſing an unconſtitutional authority and perverting their juriſdiction for the purpoſes of injuſtice and oppreſſion.

If we would wiſh for virtue in a Nation we muſt look for it in the nature of its Government. But what muſt we think of the nature of that Government which can concur in ſuch an abuſe of Parliament and ſuch a perverſion of Law and Juſtice? And what muſt we think of a Government that can join its worſt Enemies in the proſecution of an harmleſs Author, while his very Accuſers are guilty of a greater crime? An Author who

who difcovers better talents and principles for Government than many Secretaries of State that I have known. An
Author whofe hiftorical knowlege and
whofe application of political facts and
principles in Church and State are indeed
admirable; whofe temper is almoft without example; and whofe juft remarks
on the Conftitution are as important
as they are true; and fhew, much to
his honor, that he has a clear head and
an excellent heart, untainted by the
paffions of Party. He writes like a Gentleman and a Scholar; like an able and
impartial Hiftorian; and like a temperate and wife Statefman; ftating great
hiftorical facts that are indifputable; and
drawing the foundeft conclufions which
are the fineft political Leffons, and cannot be too much admired at the prefent
period in particular by our Government,
that is, by all the Conftitutional authorities of the State; for his Pamphlet is
indeed an able defence of the true principles of His Majefty's Government in
Church and State.

Whoever

Whoever the Author is he deserves a statue or *busto*. He is indisputably the most temperate, argumentative, and perfuasive political writer of the present reign. The pamphlets imputed to the late Lord Chatham are full of fire, and are written in the bold language of party for particular purposes, and are therefore only calculated for a particular period, like most short-lifed political productions; but this modest appeal to " the quiet GOOD SENSE of the Nation" is adapted to all times, and may, if our Government continues so long *unaltered*, be read with as much satisfaction a THOUSAND YEARS hence, as at present, for truth is powful and will ultimately prevail over the chicane of Lawyers and the sophistry of Statesmen. The noble Earl was a popular orator, and distinguished for the nerves attic falt and rapid eloquence of *Demosthenes*, as justly as his second fon is for the sweetnefs and profusion of *Tully*; but, although their superior eloquence charms superficial men, and gratifies the human ambition, it often fails

I   of of producing the defired and great effect, I mean the *perfuafion* which this well-informed and well-difpofed Author, produces on the minds of the candid reader, who is open to conviction, and under the influence of truth alone.

This Pamplet, though cenfured and condemned by Parliament, and even by the Government it fo ably defends, deferves to be written in characters of gold. There is indeed one flight paffage on Monarchy, which may, with a little alteration, be better explained by the Author, and which ńo man is better qualified than himfelf to do, to take out the fting of malice. Taken in its true fenfe it is unexceptionable, but perverted by the party paffions of fome men, and the ignorance of others, the meaning may be twifted to the difcredit of the Author, and to the purpofe of his enemies.

The production finely expofes the tricks of Party, that is, the hypocrify of fectaries in Church and State: IT
CUTS

CUTS SEDITION AND TREASON UP BY
THE ROOT, and produces the fineft defence of Government that has been produced by any pamphlet of the prefent
reign. But I beg the Author's pardon
for my inability to do juftice to his well-
timed and temperate appeal to " the
" quiet good Senfe of the Englifh Na-
" tion," which deferves the pen of a
JUNIUS, divefted of the party motives
of that admired writer. In that refpect
our Author is fuperior to him, for his
" Thoughts on the Englifh Government,"
though manifeftly intended as a *hafty
fketch* of a greater defign, is the moft
mafterly production of the fize that I
ever read upon our Government. He is
evidently infpired by truth, totally divefted of party paffions, and the prejudices of fectaries in Church and State,
and nobly animated in the caufe of his
country for the fecurity of His Majefty's
Government, by expofing the purita-
nical principles of modern *Jacobins* who,
like the puritans of the church, tend
equally to fedition and rebellion, and

I 2   equally

equally ftrike us with horror from tho ruinous effects of their reftlefs fpirit and poifonous doctrines.

And yet, from that fatality which often attends the nobleft works and the greateft Generals, this excellent publication is condemned by the unnatural union of the Miniftry and Oppofition in Parliament. That the Miniftry fhould join their worft enemies for fuch a purpofe, is indeed extraordinary, as I have faid it contains the moft able defence of His Majefty's Government, and is calculated to render the moft eminent fervice to good order at this period, in which the populace are running ftark mad after the delufive principles and dangerous defigns of party orators; but I do not wonder that Oppofition fhould take the alarm, and perfecute the Author for fo ably expofing their defigns, and fo effectually refuting their feditious and mifchievous principles. The Author is highly deferving the thanks and protection of Government, and of all the hatred and

malice

malice of Oppofition, for his inimitable Pamphlet, which is a Libel on the immaculate Whig-Club, and Treafon againft the factious principles of fectaries in Church and State. The production is, at this feafon of delufion and fchifm, invaluable.

Whoever would overthrow the liberty of a free Nation, muft begin by fubduing the liberty of the Prefs. All *weak* Minifters have been loud in their complaints againft the Prefs, and always have reftrained and endeavored to reftrain it. In confequence of this enmity to the Prefs, they have brow beaten writers, and punifhed them violently *againft law*. Every method has been put in practice to check the fpirit of knowledge and enquiry. But, in the prefent cafe, the information is truly flattering to Government, and of infinite fervice to adminiftration, and therefore it is the moft extraordinary, as well as the moft unufual event, that the Miniftry fhould join their worft enemies in cenfuring a production

duction fo ufeful to them, and fo injurious to the party in oppofition to their
meafures, at this period of delufion and
infatuation in which the daring efforts
of faction, like the peftilence, threaten
the very exiftence of Government.

Although no man is more attached
than myfelf to what I conceive to be the
true dignity and intereft of Executive
Government, yet I am more attached to
the Conftitution; that is, to the whole
than to any particular part of our Government. I was therefore the perfon
who advifed the difobedience of the Prin-
ters to the Houfe of Commons, becaufe
that branch of Legiflation has abfolutely no inquifitorial jurifdiction, but over
their own Members. I alfo glory in
having been the only perfon who, out
of doors had fpirit enough to oppofe the
farcical proceedings againft the late Sir
Thomas Rumbold, from a conviction
that the Houfe of Commons has not (as
Mr. Fox admits) any inquifitorial capacity
over the public. The Peers indeed, have
an

an inquifitorial power as having both a
judicial capacity (by appeal) and a legiflative one; but the Commons have not
any, as being folely legiflative, from the
nature of delegation and reprefentation;
and in no cafe whatever can it be inquifitorial, but in regard to their own
Members. The many precedents to the
contrary, are fo many inftances of an
affumed power ufurped by the Houfe of
Commons, and exercifed in breach of
the rights of the people, and the privileges of the judicial authority, or the
Laws of the Land.

As I deny this inquifitorial capacity
to the whole Houfe of Commons, fo I
condemn it *in toto* in the Secret Committee, who were by the Houfe vefted.
with an authority which I do infift the
Commons have not a right to give, becaufe it is a power by them ufurped, and
which I hope will be oppofed by my
fellow citizens with as much fpirit as I
have ever oppofed, and fhall ever oppofe
it, as a difcretionary power, not authorifed

rifed by either the Conſtitution or the
Law, and conſequently an alarming violation of the legiſlative and judicial
authorities of the Nation.

We have a memorable inſtance of
the folly of the Houſe of Commons, in
impoſing upon the public, an authority
which does not belong to them, and the
puſilanimity of the people in ſubmitting
to it in the virtuous and ſpirited conduct
of a patriotic Chief Juſtice of the King's
Bench. The Commons having made
him an *authoritative* requiſition, his Lord-
ſhip returned for anſwer, that " if the
" SPEAKER came with the whole Houſe
" of Commons in his belly, he would
" ſend him to Newgate." That honeſt
incorruptible Judge, would not have ſuf-
fered the aſſumption of a magiſterial or
inquiſitorial authority under any pretence,
but by the civil and judicial powers. To
ſhew the ſupremacy of the Law, in caſes
that affect the liberty of the ſubject, the
Chief Juſtice would not have had the
leaſt heſitation to commit any perſons,

without

without regard to their ftations, who had exercifed an improper authority over the people. In the cafe of Wilkes, the complaint was againft the illegality of the warrant from the executive power, which has no inquifitorial capacity, though it has been often exercifed by the Privy Council, and God forbid it ever fhould: For whenever the executive is armed with the civil authority, as in abfolute States, our Government, like theirs, will be arbitrary; and we fhall lofe all the bleffings of liberty, which we now happily enjoy under a moft excellent Sovereign, who deferves, equally with the immortal Roman, the glorious character of *humani generis deliciæ.*

Nor can the Parliament give to Adminiftration a power they do not poffefs themfelves; an unnatural and dangerous power in the hands of either the legiflative or executive parts of Government, fubverfive of the principles which are underftood by the Conftitution. God forbid that the inquifitorial power of

K   jurifprudence

jurifprudence fhould again be mifplaced!
It was indeed affumed and exercifed by
the STAR CHAMBER, but that ufurped
and arbitrary authority, with all its horrid
principles, has long been happily abo-
lifhed; becaufe it was of the nature of
a Catholic INQUISITION, and not congenial to our jurifprudence. The Conftitution of this Country has made a
wife diftinction between the functions of
the legiflative, the executive, the civil
and judicial powers, and on their total
feparation, depends the fecurity of civil
liberty. The doctrine of interrogatories
impofed by the ufurpation of Parliament
is the doctrine of a papifh Inquifition.

Interrogatories, in every cafe whatever,
are to be refifted, becaufe they are not
congenial to the Conftitution and Law
of the Land. They are founded on the
unfair principles of abfolute and arbitrary
Governments. There cannot be a ftronger
argument againft the horrid doctrine of
interrogatories than the exprefs prohibition
of felf-accufation, to which interrogatories,

ries, thofe efpecially of an affumed power,
lead the accufed. And fuch is the glorious bulwark of our Conftitution and
Law, that the legal authorities are
charged to admonifh the accufed, *not to
fay or to bring any thing in evidence againſt
himfelf.* So humane is the Conftitution,
fo tender is the Law of a free people,
even in the moft criminal fituation! So
abhorrent the doctrine of INTERROGA-
TORIES to a free Nation! It is the arbitrary doctrine of defpotifm.

If it be a noble, a God-like principle of
our jurifprudence, that no man fhall
accufe himfelf; it is equally a principle
of our Conftitution, that his papers fhall
not be feized to bear witnefs againſt him.
Such a *furreptitious* and violent method of
obtaining evidence, fo contrary to the
principles of our Conftitution and the
fpirit of our Laws, is an arbitrary act
congenial to an abfolute and tyrannical
Government.

I have no hefitation to fay it is a grofs

PERVERSION

PERVERSION of two Eftates of the Kingdom, neither of which has an *inquifitorial*
capacity, nor can either affume fuch a
capacity, without violating the exifting
Laws, and being guilty of *Treafon againft
the Conftitution*; a crime that is infinitely
worfe than a breach of the privileges of
Parliament complained of, which being
undefined, thofe two branches of the
Legiflature have, in too many inftances,
fhaped the Conftitution to their pleafure,
and bent it to their purpófes. This is
the language which truth infpires and
public virtue animates. It has, never-
thelefs, been obferved by an ermined
fycophant, that fuch bold truths tend to
bring into difcredit the two Houfes of
Parliament. Perifh the Judge and the
Parliament rather than fubvert the principles of our Government, by a proftitution of virtue, and a perverfion of the
Legiflature.

To prevent the error committed in
the cafe of Wilkes, for which he reco-
vered heavy damages, and by which
Lord

Lord C. J. Camden acquired immortality. Mr. Secretary Dundas was pleafed
to fay—" to avoid all doubts of the lega-
" lity of my warrant of apprehenfion,
" I affure the Houfe that it was granted
" on *information* for the feizure of papers
" containing treafonable matter." Does
that pretence conftitute the legality, and
inveft the executive with civil power
contrary to the law, and in violation of
the Conftitution? Upon the invention
of fuch an information, and under fuch
a pretence, every perfon in oppofition
to Minifters, might be fufpected and ar-
refted, upon the horrid principle of the
French revolution. It was upon infor-
mations of this fort, that the moft abfolute Governments grounded their oppref-
fions of the people; and it was a conduct
of that fort which fubverted the Government of France. God grant it may never
produce the fame revolutionary principles
in this country! To that great end it
is of the utmoft confequence to oppofe,
with Britifh fpirit and Roman virtue,
the exercife of an *inquifitorial* authority,

from

from either the Executive Power called the Privy Council, or the Legiſlative Power of the Houſe of Commons.

The greateſt enemy to our Government could not have ſuggeſted a more infidious meaſure than that adopted to iſſue WARRANTS from the Secretary of State. Such an arbitrary ſyſtem of coercion by *information* and *arreſt*, eſtabliſhes a dreadful INQUISITION in a free ſtate, more congenial to the Ruſſian than the Britiſh Nation; and, by conſequence, an abſolute Government, tending not to prevent, but to force and juſtify the revolutionary principles of France. It alarms and arms the people againſt our happy eſtabliſhments in Church and State: It forces them into a ſtate of reſiſtance in defence of their perſons, their literary property, their laws and their conſtitutional authorities: It is a bold meaſure in contempt and defiance of the Law; and is acknowledged by Miniſters themſelves, to be as illegal as it is unconſtitutional, by bringing in an

ex poſt

ex poſt faƈlo Law to make it legal. It is a renewal of the horrid principles and daring authority of the Court of STAR CHAMBER:

A juſtification of the Author of "Thoughts on the Engliſh Government," has furniſhed me with ſo much matter, that I am at a loſs for a ſeleƈtion. I am afraid of ſaying too much from its redundancy, or too little injuſtice to ſo curious a ſubjeƈt. It is ſaid that the Conſtitution is ſecretly attacked (for it is not done openly in the manner of Paine) and undermined by this Writer; and as it is the boaſt of Engliſhmen, that "it can never die," it ſhould be equally their pride to defend it. But, for the purpoſe of defence, we muſt conſider in what manner it has been attacked, and in what part it is vulnerable. The Conſtitution is in every body's mouth, and ſuch are ſuppoſed to be its noble principles and happy effeƈts, that thoſe who know nothing about it have the ſame admiration and veneration for it, as thoſe who

who are intimately acquainted with it. It is taken for granted that the Conftitution of a Free State, which has coft our anceftors fo much blood and treafure, and which is founded on the virtue and wifdom of ages, is as glorious as the fun, and as perfect as the human mind can make it. But as perfection is not to be found, and as infallibility is not the lot of human nature, this fyftem of Englifh Government is fubject, like all other things under the fun, to decay by departing from its original purity, and requiring a ferious confideration, how far the Conftitution like the Law, will admit of alteration?

As an Englifhman I do homage to the virtue and wifdom of our anceftors for framing our fyftem of Government, but I contend, that either the luxury which pervades this Nation has perverted it, or our experience of its effects from the fectarifm of a Free State fhews the neceffity of its improvement. Of its perverfion I have given melancholy inftances from the

conduct

conduct of Parliament; and of its improvement I will, after the manner of
our delicate and modeft Author, gently
offer a fpeculative opinion, and refpectfully leave it to the judgement of the
public, whofe candor and liberality of
fentiment I very much admire.

The Conftitution of this Country,
like all other human inftitutions, is to
be admired, not for its name of King,
Lords, and Commons, in which there is
nothing fupernatural, but for its principles and the happy effects they produce.
If thefe effects are fuch as were intended
by the fyftem of Government adopted by
this Nation, then it fhould be the idol
of our admiration, and it would be facri-
lege to rob it of any part of the credit
due to fo much public virtue and national
wifdom: But if experience, the parent
of wifdom, teaches that the effects are
inadequate to the great defigns of a good
Government, then it will be admitted
una voce that either the perverfion fhould
be reformed or the defect fupplied. Al-

L   though

though the perverfion and defect of the Conftitution, or Government of this Country, are words of great extent, I will flightly glance at the means of removing the one and fupplying the other: But this will be only a fpeculative and harmlefs opinion, like that of my Author, which is refpectfully fubmitted to better judges, and for which I claim a conftitutional right for myfelf and for that mafterly writer, and indeed for every fubject of a Free State, and which inherent right, congenial with the principles of our Government, I will continue to exercife unawed by the threats of any ufurped power whatever.

Our Conftitution is beautifully compared by our Author to a majeftic Oak, whofe durability, utility, and beauty are fo juftly our admiration and our boaft. But, alas! notwithftanding its remarkable durability, its unparelled utility, and its matchlefs beauty, it has the lot of human nature, which is neither immortal or infallible. Its beautiful branches will

decay

decay and it will be neceſſary to lop them off, either to ſtrengthen or preſerve the trunk. Such is the nature and ſuch the effects of our Conſtitution! The Conſtitution of the body politic is like that of the body natural: Equally ſubject to the effects of Time, they are liable to the ſame diſorders, and as the one is ſubject to amputation, ſo is the other to mutilation. The moſt violent Enemies (and violent they have been) of my Author have admitted the truth and beauty of the compariſon. They loudly call for a Reform of Parliament, which ſhews that the Conſtitution is perverted or there would be no occaſion to reform it. If they admit of the abuſe of their own power, with what propriety can they blame other men for being of the ſame opinion ? It is that perverſion or abuſe, call it which you pleaſe, that renders the ſyſtem imperfect and the effect inadequate. If that imperfection is generally admitted the difference of opinion is only in the means of reformation. I have as much right as any man to give

an

an opinion on reforming the Conftitution as Party-men on the reform of
any one branch of it. Upon this fubject,
fo important to a free Nation, the Sen-
timents of a Free and enlightened people
will be as different as their complexions;
and yet they have an equal right of
thinking and of giving a fpeculative opinion provided it does not injure the eftablifhed Government, which injury (not
allowed by any Government) is produced
by pofitive and bold affertions like thofe
of Paine and other avowed Enemies, and
not by fpeculative opinions of the beft
friends to the Laws and to the Conftitution.

The Gentleman-like Author of this
much abufed Pamphlet, feems to prefer
a monarchical Government, which is the
Government of this Country, and fo do
I. I do not *fay*, as that able Writer feems
to *think*, that I prefer a Government that
is purely monarchical, but I contend that
he has a right to admire it if it ftrikes his
mind to be the beft fyftem of Government,

ment. It is evident that he is unfriendly to a Republican Government, and
therefore he cannot be accufed, like fome
great men in Parliament that I have in
my eye, of being an Advocate for the
prefent mad fyftem of Equality and Fra-
ternity, that threatens the total overthrow of our Conftitution. If he is
blameable for inclining rather too much to
unlimited monarchy, they are criminal
for daringly efpoufing the caufe of democracy, and endangering that conftitutional fyftem of Government which they
fo much affect to admire.

I endeavour to avoid thefe extremes
by contending for a Government that is
neither one or the other. A fyftem that
is not totally monarchical or republican,
but a limited Monarchy confifting of
both, Neither abfolute monarchy or a
Government purely republican is congenial to the Genius of this Nation, or
conducive to its true intereft. It muft be
a mixed Government that happily com-
bines the dignity and efficacy of the monarchical

narchical, with the principles of the Republican, and is called a Monarchy regulated by Laws, to diftinguifh it from an abfolute Monarchy, acting from the will of the Sovereign. This is my humble opinion, other men have a right to the opinion that moft forcibly ftrikes their minds, without the imputation of being unfriendly to our Government, or to the privileges of any one branch of the Legiflature, commonly called the Conftitution.

When our Anceftors gave us a Conftitution, founded on the concurrence and co-operation of three Branches, and called them King, Lords, and Commons, if they wifhed to render the principles of their fyftem eternal, they did not expect the forms, like the fpirit, to be immutable. If the noble principles are preferved, and the happy effects are produced, I think it is immaterial, what name or fhape it takes. I am a great admirer of the dignity, the energy, and effect of monarchical Government; and not withftanding ſtanding the dreadful examples we have had of its abuſe, I ſhould prefer a Government intirely monarchical, could we always be ſure of ſuch an excellent Monarch as now adorns the Throne, and ſuch a Miniſtry as now ſo ably conducts the affairs of this Nation: But as theſe bleſſings are uncertain, the Genius and the intereſt of this country require a mixed Government, or a monarchy limited by the Laws of the Land. This concluſion leads me from the favourite idea of my modeſt Author to my own opinion of a limited Monarchy.

Luxury, which like a torrent, pervades Europe; Luxury which is both a great bleſſing and a great curſe (a bleſſing to a manufacturing Nation by its induſtry, and a curſe by perverting the Conſtitution and the Law) has had a manifeſt effect upon our ſyſtem of Government. Can it then be wondered that this Conſtitution, which is ſapped by luxury, the parent of corruption and proſtitution, ſhould be compared by ingenious men to the

the royal oak, whofe beautiful branches are decayed by time, and lopped off by neceffity? This ingenious comparifon, which is as modeft as it is true, does not, in the leaft, attack the privileges of any one branch of our Conftitution. He may fay, with his amiable Sovereign, *Honi foit qui mal y penfe.* But had he faid that the branches of the Conftitution, like thofe of a Tree, fhould be lopped off whenever they become corrupt or ufelefs, he would have faid a truth, ftrictly within the right given him by the Conftitution, and the Law; fince it does not affect the Government nor violate the Law. I am fo much convinced that Englifhmen poffefs this natural and conftitutional right to advance a fpeculative opinion, that, even under the perfecution of the Author of "Thoughts "on the Englifh Government," I will venture to deliver my opinion upon a fyftem moft congenial to the temper, and moft conducive to the intereft of this commercial Nation.

I have

I have faid that I admire a well-judged union between a monarchical and a republican fyftem of Government, in which the dignity and efficiency of the one is founded on the principles and energy of the other, to the end that the fupremacy of the Crown may be conducive to the true happinefs of the people: For the felicity of the fubject is the true intereft of the Monarch. The dignity of the one is infeparable from the profperity of the other. This I am confident is the opinion of our incomparable Sovereign, and the opinion alfo of his excellent Minifters.

Should TIME produce an alteration in our Conftitution (for Time changes all things) I apprehend it will be in the ariftocratic branch. That is the branch which I think can be beft difpenfed with, confiftent with the principles of a mixed Government and the purity of national liberty. The ariftocracy may be confidered more as the appendage of Monarchy than as a diftinct branch of the

M   Conftitution.

Conſtitution. Peers are the Creatures and generally the *echo* of Sovereignty. It is no ſolecifm to ſay it is the very creature of its Creator. If ever Peers are in oppoſition it is becauſe their ambition is not ſufficiently gratified. Titles, Ribbands, Feathers and Toys, often inſpire the virtue and animate the wiſdom of this branch of the Engliſh Government. It conſiſts of two parts, ſpiritual and temporal, equally eager to gratify their ambition and venality. Ariſtocracy is the bane of every Monarchy, and a libel on the equal rights and liberty of this Nation: The ambition and the imperious influence of this order are the greateſt misfortunes of a free State. Ariſtocracy is not congenial to liberty. In my apprehenſion that branch of the Conſtitution may be well ſpared without any injury to our ſyſtem of Government; which I contend will be more perfect by lopping off the great ſource of national corruption and political proſtitution, which, like the peſtilence, infects the democratic order, and threatens, by its

ambition

ambition and overbearing influence on the legiſlative and executive powers, to rouſe the people to conſtitutional re-ſiſtance.

Ariſtocracy is a *privileged* order incom-patable with a free State, in which the Nobles and the .dignified Clergy have more influence then is conſiſtent with national liberty and the public intereſt. Ariſtocracy is incompatible with the rights and intereſts of mankind. It is a ſcourge to the ſubjects of arbitrary Go-vernments, and the greateſt evil in a free Nation. Indeed it is a deſcription of men that offers an indignity to civilized hu-man nature, and a groſs inſult to Li-berty. If its proud diſtinction inſults our underſtandings and our feelings, its effects upon Government offer a ſtill greater inſult to the wiſdom, the ſpirit, and liberty of the Age. What are the greateſt curſes in all arbitrary Govern-ments? Ariſtocracy and the dignified Clergy. What occaſioned the Revolution in France? Ariſtocracy and the dignified

M 2   Clergy.

clergy. What is the greateſt ſolecifm in the Britiſh Government? The privileged order of Ariſtocracy, confiſting of the Nobles and the dignified Clergy. A *Legiſlative* Ariſtocracy is the greateſt ſolecifm in a Nation diſtinguiſhed for civil Liberty. Mankind are well acquainted with Monarchical and Republican Government, but Ariſtocratical principles are a ſort of policy repugnant to both. It will be ſaid that Ariſtocracy in a free State is not a diſtinct power over the people (or the Government of the Nobles) but wiſely bounded on the one ſide by the monarchical, and on the other ſide by the democratical part of our Conſtitution. Admitted; and *ſo far* if it did not do much good it might not do much miſchief. But the misfortune is its influence exceeds its bounds, abſorbs the democracy in the vortex of its all-powerful effects, and occaſions all the evils which ariſe from ambition, luxury, corruption, and proſtitution. The bleſſings of a wiſe Monarchy are like the inundation of the Nile that manures and fertiliſes the land; but

but the calamitous pride of Ariftocracy
is like the overflowing of great rivers
that wafh away the farmers toil and fte-
rilize the land.   ·

The powerful afcendency in Church
and State of this proud Order of the Nation (which infults human nature and
degrades the human underftanding by
an imperious fuperiority) may one day or
other render it neceffary to lop off the
ariftocratic branch of the Legiflature,
which I am perfuaded can be done without any injury to our Conftitution, but
on the contrary, with the greateft con-
fiftency and advantage to our limited
Monarchy, which will continue a mixed
Government by dividing it equally between the regal and democratic powers,
a fyftem that will have more energy and
a happier effect. The Ariftocracy is only
neceffary to the influence of the Crown,
and to the gratification of their own ambition. In its legiflative capacity its authority is nominal depending on the
pleafure of its Creator. A Ribband, or
the

the diſtinction of a title will gratify ariſtocratic ambition, influence their conduct, and decide the fate of this Nation,
and perhaps of Europe.

The Ariſtocratic branch of our Conſtitution poſſeſſes a judicial authority not
in the firſt inſtance as a Court of Law,
but by appeal as a Court of Equity.
This power may be as ſafely lodged with
the democratic as with the ariſtocratic
part of Government, and perhaps with
a better effect, inaſmuch as it may rea-
ſonably be ſuppoſed that a great number
in one Houſe poſſeſs a greater ſhare of
wiſdom and virtue than a ſmaller number
in the other Houſe of Parliament.

Should the utility of Ariſtocracy in a
free State be inſiſted upon, I would aſk
in what does it conſiſt? Does it give efficacy to our Laws or energy to our Government? It is in rank the ſecond order,
but it is the mere *echo* of the firſt. Nor
do I ſcruple to ſay that Ariſtocracy is not
a bleſſing to any Government. It is not
congenial

congenial to a fyftem of liberty. Its influence over the people's fhare of the Conftitution is the caufe of all thofe evils which require a *reform* in that branch of the Legiflature, and which may go near to fubvert the Conftitution.

The following are a few of the many inftances of this truth. "The Duke of " Norfolk has now purchafed as many " Burgage Tenures as give him a majority " over Lady Irwin at Horfham: The " whole number which gives the right " of Election for this Borough is twenty- " five."

The Duke of Devonfhire influences the return of one member for the County, and one for the town of Derby, and nominates two for the manufacturing town of Knarefborough, where the right of election is in the Burgage-holds, and the Burgage-holds, eighty-eight in number, belong all to the Duke.

The Duke of Marlborough carries

one

one for the County and another for the City of Oxford, nominates one for the Village of Heytefbury, where the fifty Burgage-holds which have the right of Election are the moiety of them, the property of his Grace; and the other moiety the property of Mr. A'Court. His Grace has alfo the nomination of two more reprefentatives for the Manor of Woodftock.

The Duke of Rutland is a minor, and his Election intereft, for the prefent, is managed by his guardians, Mr. Pitt and the Duke of Beaufort.

Bramber, in Suffex, which place confifts of eighteen thatched houfes at the bottom of a ftreet, the top of which is another Borough, called Steyning, which together fend four members to reprefent the people. Steyning belongs half to the Duke of Norfolk, and half to Sir John Honeywood. Bramber is half the property of the Duke of Rutland, and the other half belongs to Sir Henry Calthorpe.

thorpe. Grantham and Newark, which each fend one under the fame influence, make it eight. This is a number equalled only by Lord Lonfdale, and exceeded only by the Duke of Norfolk.

Thefe are only a few of the many inftances of the afcendency, nay, of the fovereign power of the Ariftocracy over the Democracy. And when we confider the vaft influence of the whole Body of Peers and alfo of the Executive Power, may we not fay that the Reprefentatives of the People are more properly the Reprefentatives of their political Creators? And may we not, with equal truth, fay that one Houfe of Parliament dependent on the Crown, and the other dependent on the Peers, form together a ftrange fort of popular Reprefentation? A reprefentation which difcovers a great defect in the principle of the popular part of our Government, and as great a caufe of refiftance to the alarming power affumed by the Houfe of Commons, not congenial to the delegation of an autho-

N   rity

rity which is intirely legiflative. The functions of every Branch of the Legiflature are highly refpectable, and fhould ever be confidered with the homage which national authority requires, to produce the energy and happy effects of Government; but whenever thofe functions are perverted or abufed, by affuming an authority incompatible with legiflation, they lofe the refpect that is fo neceffary to the dignity and energy of Government. The afcendency of the fecond over the third Eftate of the Kingdom through their rank and landed property, and the powerful intereft it gives them in the Nation, places the reft of the people at fo great a diftance as may one day roufe them to a juft fenfe of the vaft inequality of their condition. The luxury of this imperious order, and the *Vaffallage* of the induftrious and moft numerous part of a manufacturing Nation is thus emphatically and truly defcribed: " The Lord *within* fits in ftate, revelling, " banqueting and tantalizing the palled " appetite; while the wretch *without*, re-
pulfed

" pulfed, infulted, and refufed his due,
" is perhaps perifhing with hunger."

Should what I have faid put me under
the difpleafure of the Houfe of Lords, I
fhall not be convinced by any threats
that I am diforderly; nor fhall I, like the
daftardly witneffes examined by the Houfe
of Commons, rafhly furrender the rights
of my fellow-fubjects, by acknowledging
the inquifitorial capacity of Parliament,
and anfwering to any interrogatories:
This fidelity is what I owe to myfelf, to
my Country, and to the Laws, or to
the Judicial Power, to which alone every
offender is amenable.

Although I wifh to fee fuch a Reform
as fhall divide the Conftitution between
the regal and democratic powers, forming
a mixed Government, partly monarchical
and partly republican, I am far from
meaning that the democratic branch of
the Legiflature does not want reform.
Luxury, ambition and venality, have not
fown the feeds of corruption and profti-

tution

tution in one branch only. Nothing can
fo effectually reform this branch, which is
infeparable from the *limited* monarchy of a
Free State, as lopping off the other which
has fo great an influence over it, and fo
lordly a power over the landed property and
intereft of the Nation. Placemen muft
ever hold their rank in the Legiflature
as the beft acquainted with the various
branches of Executive Government. Admitting their conduct to be influenced by
their places, it is a defect that feems to
be inevitable. The fame may be faid of
Contractors. Thefe are evils natural to
a great commercial State, and infeparable
from the beft Government. The only
clafs of men that I would exclude, is
the race of Lawyers, who, like the Locufts
in Egypt, that ate up every green thing,
devour the Conftitution. The influence
of this part of the public is truly alarming, and we are abfolutely as much Law-
ridden, as the moft bigotted Catholic
country is Prieft-ridden. Employed to
every purpofe, and adopting every principle conducive to their venality, they
fubftitute

fubftitute the practice of the Old Bailey for the principles of the Conftition, and proftituting their legiflative like their judicial opinions for the purpofes of ambition and venality, they poifon the fprings of the Legiflature, and make the Laws a terror to the people. The difqualification of this venal and unabafhed clafs of men, and the admiffion of the Clerical order, feems to be the only reform neceffary to the Houfe of Commons. Whether reprefentation be for feven or three years, it will be immaterial whenever the influence of Ariftocracy and the afcendancy of Lawyers are removed. I do therefore moft heartily wifh for a total extinction of the humiliating and vaft influence of the ariftocracy and the dignified clergy, and the difqualification of Lawyers in the Houfe of Commons.

It is truly faid, that " Lawyers twift " words and meanings as they pleafe." The conduct of Mr. Erfkine illuftrates this truth. The Hon. Gentleman, who is fo much admired for his legal talents,

is

is the firſt to violate the Law which he is ſuppoſed to underſtand ſo well. As Chairman of the Whig-Club, he has been the firſt to violate, in the moſt public manner, the Act againſt ſeditious aſſemblies, tending to miſguide the people, and endanger His Majeſty's Government. The publication of their deſign is an act of hoſtility againſt the ſtatute intended for the ſuppreſſion of ſuch Aſſociations. I appeal to Mr. Erſkine, who ſo well underſtands the Law, whether his conduct and that of his aſſociates, are not in defiance of the Act, and a manifeſt violation of it. For inſtance: " Reſolved that it is the opinion of this " Meeting, that an Aſſociation ſhould be " forthwith formed for the purpoſe of " procuring, by all *legal* means, the repeal " of the Acts deſcribed; and of *reſtoring* " to the ſubjects of this Country, the " full benefit of the proviſions in the " BILL of RIGHTS." This contains a falſe charge againſt Government; a falſe alarm to the public; and a falſe method of redreſs. As an eminent lawyer, the Hon.

Hon. Gentleman knows that fuch Affociations are become illegal, and confe-
quently they cannot be the legal means
of redrefs. They are directly in the teeth
of the Act, and the idea of reftoring the
rights of the people, implies their being
wrefted from them by the Legiflature,
a charge which the Parliament will not
admit. The only legal means of procuring the repeal of an Act which is fuppofed to trench on the rights of the
people, is through the channel of the
Conftituent branch of the public, and
not through Affociations which are de-
clared illegal.

Such is my opinion of the impropriety
and illegality of thefe rafh means of ftir-
ring up the people, againft the neceffary
meafures of Government for the public
fecurity at a very dangerous period, that
were I in the Commiffion of the Peace
for Middlefex, where the Affociation is
held, I fhould think it a duty I owe to
the Laws and to the Peace of my Country, to apprehend every perfon who
called

called the Meeting contrary to Law, and in defiance of the ſtatute, without diſtinction, for it is a diſtinguiſhing feature of His Majeſty's Government, and the peculiar happineſs of a free people, that the higheſt equally with the loweſt ranks of ſociety, are amenable to the judicial autority for offences againſt the law.

To cloſe my remarks on the Pamphlet entitled " Thoughts on the Engliſh Go-" vernment," which is a well-timed and judicious appeal to " the quiet GOOD " SENSE of the Britiſh Nation;" I contend that the context will not juſtify the concluſion drawn by his accuſers of his evil intentions to the Conſtitution. But admitting the facts were ſtated with a manifeſt deſign to apply them againſt the two Houſes of Parliament; what is the nature of the Author's crime, and what is the authority of Parliament in this caſe? Has he injured any one branch of the Legiſlature to weaken the Government, or has he violated any Law? Will any man ſay that the ſpeculative opinion

of

of an hiftorical writer, both inconclufive and harmlefs, is a Libel on the two branches of the Conftitution called the Parliament, or that it is a Libel on the Revolution which is an imaginary thing?

Suppofe the writer means that the *three* Eftates of the Kingdom might be compreffed into *one*, without any injury to the energy and efficacy of Government, is there any crime againft the Law of the Land in advancing fuch a fpeculative opinion? He does not fay, in the manner of Paine, that it *fhould* be, or *muft* be, as neceffary to the beft Government; but that it *might* be without any injury to this Government. But fuppofing his opinion of our Conftitution contained all the culpability and criminality which have been difcovered by certain Statefmen, who feel fore, what authority have the two Houfes of Parliament over this reputed literary criminal? Does the Houfe of Commons, as a part of the Legiflature, poffefs an inquifitorial capacity to erect itfelf into a

o   political

political Tribunal in the manner of a Catholic Inquifition, or the Houfe of Lords a judicial capacity to fit in judgement on the accufation of this Heretical Inquifition? Certainly not. Then *cui bono?*

I have repeatedly obferved, without fear of contradiction, that the two branches are purely legiflative, except in cafes of appeal when the Lords exercife a judicial authority, but the power of the Commons is totally legiflative in all cafes whatfoever. Whenever they erect themfelves into an Inquifition and examine witneffes at their ufurped Tribunal, on which to ground a charge againft His Majefty's Subjects, they abufe their legiflative authority, as in the prefent cafe, and violate the Conftitution infinitely more than the Author of " Thoughts on the Englifh Government."

" The power of the Commons, it muft be confeffed, is at prefent much more confiderable than in former reigns; and it it appears from Henry Eighth's application to the Barons for a fupply, that he did not confider the Commons as the *fole* Reprefentatives of the people." Whether this was a mark of Royal difpleafure againft the one Houfe, or of greater confidence in the other, the application was as impolitic as it was wrong. But notwithftanding the propriety of Money Bills originating with the Houfe of Commons it is no proof of an exclufive and fole right to that greateft of all Acts, namely the granting fupplies to the King for the purpofes of Executive Government. It fhould feem from the name of Parliament, and its fitting in two different houfes or diftinct chambers, as a check on each other (for that is the great object of a mixed Government) that they are equally a reprefentative power and have equal rights in every meafure of Legiflation, that of granting fupplies for the public fervice in particular, as being of the moft confequence.

From what caufe the Commons have

fo

fo confiderably increafed their power, or upon what principle it is maintained I cannot conceive; fince both the fovereign power it exercifes in the above inftance, and its affumed inquifitorial capacity are unwarrantable, and fubverfive of the Conftitution, by deftroying that equipoife or nice *equilibrium* which is the beauty of our mixed Government. But whatever was the original defign of Parliaments, or whatever is at prefent the principle of the two branches of the Legiflature, it is manifeft that our Government is monarchical and will probably continue fuch, though the conftitutional Tree fhould be fhorn of its branches; becaufe Monarchy is a fyftem of Government moft congenial to the temper and fpirit of the people, and moft conducive to the dignity and intereft of this Nation.

In defending this Author, I appeal to God for the purity of my intentions, and to my Country for the truth of my remarks. The Writings of Paine were founded on ignorance and malice to our Government:

Government: they were like the peſtilence to our Conſtitution. They were a
bare-faced attack, tending to occaſion a
Revolution for the total overthrow of our
Government. The writings of this well-
informed Author are of a different nature,
tending to produce a contrary effect by
promoting the beſt pupoſes of His Majeſty's Government. He neither attacks
the Conſtitution or violates the Law. In
the moſt exceptionable paſſage of the production, he only glances at an idea that
is not half ſo exceptionable as the ſpeculative opinions of the Duke of Richmond
and Mr. Pitt, which were bold and radi-
cal innovations. I am as warm an advocate as any man for the neceſſary dignity
of authority, but let me tell the Houſe
of Commons that their privileges are of
a legiſlative and not of a judicial nature.
Whenever the people are ſuppoſed to
offend, ſo as to affect the Government of their Country, the Executive
Power, by an appeal to the Judicial Authority, will make them amenable to the
Laws of the Land, to be dealt with
according

according to the nature of the offence in the judgement of their Peers, and not in the judgement of either of the two Houſes of Parliament.

Our Conſtitution is a mighty convenient thing, it being equally the hobby-horſe of Friends and Foes: The Executive Power is jealous of the Conſtitution; the Parliament is jealous of the Conſtitution; and the People are jealous of the Conſtitution. Surely this Conſtitution muſt have ſingular principles and heterogeneous properties that Friends and Foes ſhould rally round it! The Parliament, tenacious of their ſhare of the Conſtitution, complain of a breach of their privileges and proceed to pronounce judgement in their own cauſe!!! In the manner of an arbitrary Tribunal they are Judges and Jury in their own caſe. They forget, that according to the Laws, *they* have made, they muſt ſhew what their privileges are, and in what manner they are affected. This is all that concerns the Houſe of Commons: For ſhould it

be

be deemed by the Laws of the Land (through the Judicial Authority) to be a fcandalous and feditious Libel on the Government of this Country, tending to alienate the affections of His Majefty's fubjects, and to fubvert the true principles of the Conftitution, the Parliament has nothing to do with the crime. I have juft obferved, that whenever the Conftitution is libelled, Executive Government will appeal to the Laws, and make the offender amenable to the Judicial Power, and not to the Legiflative Authority of Parliament. The pre-examination and pre-judgement of the Houfe of Commons is contrary to the principles and practice of the Courts of Law, a violation of the rights of the people, and a high breach of the privileges of the Judicial Authority to which the cafe exclufively belongs.

There are indeed inftances in which our Conftitution has been attacked, and it became neceffary to repel the attack for the dignity of Government; but that was done according to Law by the Judicial Power.

Power. The Commons may fuppofe an Author guilty of a breach of their privileges and cenfure him for it, but they have no right to pronounce him guilty of " a fcandalous and feditious Libel, tend-" ing to alienate the affections of the " people from His Majefty's Government " and fubvert the Conftitution;" a fentence which belongs entirely to the Judicial Authority: And as it is an high crime againft Government, the charge, like other cafes of fedition, fhould come from the Executive and not from the Legiflative Power, and be brought into a Court of Law, and not before the Houfe of Lords, as was firft intended, and which is not right in any cafe whatever: It was not right in the cafe of Haftings, who, if amenable to any Court of Juftice in Europe, was amenable to the Judicial Authority only in my apprehenfion.

If Parliament wifh for an inftance of fedition tending to alienate the affections of the people from His Majefty's Perfon and Government, I have given them one

in

in the conduct of Oppofition in both
Houfes of Parliament, and I will repeat
it. The conduct of the Duke of Bedford,
in contending for the univerfal Rights of
the People (like the univerfal Suffrage of
the Duke of Richmond) to affemble and
petition the Legiflature, difcovers great
ignorance of our Conftitution, by which
the rights of the collective body are totally abforbed by the conftituent part of
the people: So that the invitation to
roufe and render active the great mafs of
the people, is the moft alarming attack
on the Conftitution, and the moft dangerous refiftance to Executive Government. The conduct of his Grace is a
greater Libel on His Majefty's Government than that complained of by Mr.
Sheridan. The conduct of the Earl of
Albemarle in the cafe of the Author of
" Thoughts on the Englifh Government,"
though not equally culpable with his
Grace, is equally erroneous and fubverfive of juftice and liberty. His Lordfhip
applying the moft exceptionable paffage,
without confidering the context, to the

P   privileges

privileges of the ariftocratic part of our
Conftitution, has pronounced it a Libel
on that Houfe of Parliament, and made
a motion for that purpofe which was
very properly rejected, becaufe, had the
complaint been founded, it would have
been inconfiftent with every idea of juftice, to pronounce judgement upon it in
the very jurifdiction into which it was
expected to be carried judicially. How
could the accufed expect juftice when
his cafe had been prejudged and decided
againft him, contrary to the principles
and practice of every court of juftice?

To conclude: That a pamphlet ob-
vioufly written for the falutary purpofes
of good order in the very worft times,
and manifeftly calculated to produce that
happy effect by co-operating with the
ftrong but neceffary meafures of the Legiflature; I fay that fuch a production
in defence of Government, fhould be
pronounced by Parliament to be a feditious Libel is really aftonifhing, nay, it
is a monftrous folecifm. But inftead of
its

its being " a malicious, fcandalous and
" feditious Libel, to create jealofies and
" and divifions among His Majefty's fub-
" jects, to alienate their affections from
" his Government and to fubvert the
" true principles of the Conftitution," I
have fhewn that it is the REVERSE. I
have fhewn that it is a fine panegyric on
His Majefty's Government founded on
the true principles of our Conftitution
and Law, tending to cement the affections and refpect of the People for His
Majefty's Perfon and Government, and
to deftroy fedition and divifions by a temperate and juditious appeal to " the quiet
GOOD SENSE of the Nation."

If it is a Libel or Treafon it is againft
the immaculate Whig-Club and the hy-
pocritical Sectaries in Church and State.
No wonder then that the Members of
that Club, in both Houfes of Parliament,
fhould move Heaven and Earth to accufe
and condemn the Author *extrajudicially*:
But it is a wonder indeed, that the Miniftry fhould be duped into their opinion

" of

" of *the new and sublime destiny that awaits*
" *their fellow creatures*," and be drawn in
to co-operate with their worst enemies in
their worst design.

I honor Mr. Sheridan for very properly moving, that a Pamphlet which so
ably proves the hypocrisy of his party,
and so happily exposes the seditious principles of his deluded adherents (which
at this moment threaten the overthrow
of His Majesty's Government) should be
burnt by the common hangman; but
Mr. Dundas is the first Minister of this
Country, who ever proposed that the
Author of an inimitable production, ma-
nifestly calculated to crush sedition at a
dangerous period, (to whom he confessed
the public were indebted for the peace
and security which were now enjoyed in
this Country) and to quiet the minds of
the people for the best purposes of His
Majesty's Government, should be prose-
cuted by Government, for a Libel on the
Jacobin system of opposition !

To

To acknowledge in Parliament the Author's great merit, at the moft alarming period, and his great claim to the admiration of Government for fo fingular a fervice, which gives him a title to a recompence from His Majefty, and with the fame breath for a Secretary of State to petition His Majefty to profecute that very Author for a Pamphlet fo ufeful to the purpofes of Government, is indeed a monftrous folecifm, and the greateft abfurdity and injuftice that ever was heard from the Executive Power of this Country. To profecute your beft Friend, upon a falfe charge, at the requeft of your worft Enemies, for the very great fervices done you to defeat their ruinous purpofes, is a LIBEL on the virtue of the Legiflature, and TREASON againft the wifdom and juftice of His Majefty's Government.

Happily for that Author and myfelf we live in the mild reign of one of our beft Princes, whofe public virtue is equal

to

to the righteous adminiftration of *Titus,
Nerva, Trajan, Aurelius,* &c. of whofe
bleffed time *Tacitus* fays, with extacy,
*Rara temporum felicitate, ubi fentire quæ velis,
& quæ fentias dicere liceat.*

APPENDIX.

HAVING kept back the prefs through the Recefs of Parliament, it gives me an opportunity totake a little notice of one of the moft
extraordinary publications that I ever met with
from a Statefman of Mr. Fox's fplendid talents,
great political experience, deep knowledge of our
Conftitution and Law, acute penetration and mafterly judgement. After fubfcribing *ex animo* to
the fplendor of his talents, and doing him the
juftice to fay, that much as I admire the fweetnefs
and profufion of *Tully* in Mr. Pitt, I am charmed
with the nerves, attic falt, and rapid eloquence of
Demofthenes which diftinguifh this popular orator,
facred truth requires me to fay that I am the more
aftonifhed at the impolitic production, in the pro-
portion that I admit the brilliancy of his abilities,

a   and

and the vaſt effect which his powerful exertions
have produced on the public mind. I have been
twenty years attentive to the perſuaſive eloquence
of the Right Hon. Gentleman; and, as I am in
the liberal habit of imputing the beſt motives
to men in public ſtations, I give him credit
for his good intentions; but that is, in the preſent and other inſtances, at the expence of his
judgement: For he often maintains principles,
which I will do him the juſtice to admit, he does
not believe himſelf. Had I not known more of Mr.
Fox than his preſent ill-judged and ill-timed publication, I ſhould have thought him either an idiot
or a madman: For none but an idiot or a man
wrong in his head, would have publiſhed ſuch a
production, at ſuch a period, in which this
Country and all Europe, ſtake the exiſtence of
their Governments on the tranquillity of the
People.

"The DECLARATION of the WHIG-CLUB,"
(beſides it being greatly to be lamented at this
period in which all Nations are convulſed, and
all Governments ſhaken to their foundations by
ſimilar declarations (is a declaration of Treaſon
againſt the Conſtitution and the Law. "A ſo-
"ciety of men feel themſelves bound to propoſe
"a great national meaſure to the people." If
Mr.

Mr. Fox has the face to fay, he will not have the
courage to fhew, that any fociety or body of men
whatever have a right, from the Conftitution,
to propofe fuch a meafure. Were this right admitted, it would not only deftroy the exclufive
right of the Conftituent body to petition, but it
would fubvert the Legiflative and Executive
Powers of the State. He has the candor to con-
fefs "the meafure is unufual, becaufe it can be
" juftified by no ordinary circumftances;" nor, I
will add, upon any principle known to the Conftitution and Law of this Country. The attempt
is, therefore, congenial to the French revolution;
and as it can be juftified upon no other principle,
the contagion fhould be refifted as early and with
as much care, as we would guard againft the
introduction of the peftilence.

" WE think the fituation of this Country no
" longer permits us to confide the fupport of our
" principles, to the individual exertions of our
" Members." *Rifum teneatis amici!* Who are
we and *us?* Do the principles which they are
unwilling to truft, proceed from any body of His
Majefty's Subjects known to our Conftitution?
The man who can write in this manner muft, to
borrow an expreffion of the great Mansfield, be
" wrong in his head." " The Whig-Club in-

" variably

" variably adhering to the principles of the
" Britifh Conftitution, as eftablifhed at the Revo-
" lution, cannot be *unconcerned* fpectators of the
" deftruction of the moft important fecurities of
" public liberty, which were provided at that
" glorious *æra.*" Good God! Is it poffible that
a Statefman of Mr. Fox's rank can be guilty of
fuch an expreffion, as " unconcerned fpectators?"
Is he aware of the magnitude and tendency of the
expreffion? Of the effect it may produce, under
the critical circumftances of our Country, on the
minds of the public to the injury of Government? The Author of " Thoughts on the Englifh Government" has fhewn, with great ability
and perfpicuity, the true principles and defigns,
from time to time, of the Whig-Club; and has,
in a happy ftile, expofed the folly of thofe who
pin their political faith on the duplicity and ver-
fatility of Party. He has happily ridiculed the
principles fuppofed to be eftablifhed at the glorious æra of the Revolution, from the cleareft
evidence, that this Nation had no Revolution
at all in 1688, or at any fubfequent *epocha.* To
this I have added, that the famous Bill of Rights,
fo often referred to with extacy, as a vaft acquifition of liberty, was only an *explanatory* Bill of
Rights inherent in our Government, either not fo
clearly explained or fo fully underftood before,
but

but no real addition to civil liberty. As explanatory acts are fometimes neceffary to the better underftanding of our Laws, fo this definition of the Conftitution was found neceffary to the clear comprehenfion and fatisfaction of the people, who have ever fince thought it a vaft fecurity of their rights, derived from a Revolution which abfolutely had not the fhadow of exiftence.

The Whig-Club, therefore, founding its principles upon an imaginary event muft, as a neceffary confequence, maintain principles as vifionary as its foundation, and as delufive; and therefore it became neceffary, from time to time, to cajole that part of the public, who look no further than the furface of pompous political profeffions. The prefent is an inftance of this truth, fo palpable and fo grofs, that I think it offers the greateft infult to the virtue as well as to the underftanding of the Nation. Mr. Fox fays "the Whig-Club "cannot be unconcerned fpectators of the def- "truction of the moft important fecurities of "public liberty." If this means any thing, it is that they are armed and invite the people to arm themfelves, in the language of the French revolution, to make a ftand againft "the deftruction "of the moft important fecurities of Civil "Liberty.

The

The orator would have dealt fairly with Executive Government if he had fhewn what important fecurities he alluded to, and in what manner they have been deftroyed; fince it does not appear, from any thing he has faid of the Bills lately enacted, nor indeed can it be believed from their receiving the approbation of fo great a part of the Legiflature, and the concurrence of the *real fenfe* of the Nation. Without fuch a demonftration the charge muft appear malicious, and feditious, tending to criminate the conduct of Parliament, to deftroy the confidence of the people, and to alienate their affections from His Majefty's Government. I am as bold as I am happy to fay, without fear of contradiction, that this heavy charge, fo unjuft in its nature, and fo impolitic and dangerous, at this period, in its operation on the minds of the public, has not the leaft foundation in truth; nor any exiftence but in the principles and views of party, to perplex the Legiflative and Executive Powers of the Nation, at a time in which every heart fhould wifh, and every head endeavor to give energy and effect to His Majefty's Government.

" The deftruction of the moft important fe-" curities of public liberty" is an untruth, that conveys the fevereft reflection and indeed the
heavieft

heavieſt charge on the much-admired reign of
our moſt amiable Sovereign, who is equal in private goodneſs and in public virtue to the moſt
celebrated of the Roman Princes. I have obſer-
ved, with extacy, that the principles of religious
and civil Liberty have been better underſtood,
and, by conſequence, better ſecured by the illuſtrious Houſe of Hanover than by any former
Princes who have ſat upon the Throne of this
Kingdom. The groundleſs charge, therefore,
does the greateſt injuſtice to the mild and happy
reign of a Monarch, whoſe ſplendid virtues ex-
alt human nature, and whoſe invariable and exem-
plary regard for true Religion and ſubſtantial
Juſtice, deſerves immortality. By modeſtly defending the character of this illuſtrious Prince,
I mean to pay a juſt tribute of praiſe to his Miniſters for adviſing His Majeſty to meaſures which
are ſo far from " deſtroying the moſt important
" ſecurities of the Nation," that they have given
the beſt ſecurity to the liberty and property of
the ſubject, by preventing a political contagion
that would have brought upon this country, all
the terror and calamity that have diſtreſſed France
and endangered all Europe.

" The Conſtitution can," in the judgement
of Mr. Fox and his adherents, " now only be
" reſtored

" *reſtored* by the exerciſe of that juſt authority,
" which the national opinion muſt ever poſſeſs,
" over the proceedings of the Legiſlature." But
I maintain there is no occaſion to *reſtore* a Conſtitution which I have ſhewn has not been violated,
and which, I may venture to ſay, will never be
violated by the illuſtrious Family on the Throne:
It has, at leaſt, the greateſt ſecurity at preſent
in the Virtues of the Sovereign and the wiſdom
of His Majeſty's Miniſters. But were we to
ſuppoſe it violated and our liberties in danger,
" the exerciſe of an authority, which the nati-
" onal opinion muſt always poſſeſs, over the
" proceedings of the Legiſlature," is an authority
that only exiſts in the diſtempered imagination
of Party-men, who are ever in oppoſition to the
meaſures of Government, right or wrong, and
who would have no political conſequence without throwing obſtacles in the way of Adminiſtra-
tion.

The opinion of the real Public will ever have
great weight with both the legiſlative and executive powers of the Nation, when that opinion is
known through the conſtituent part of the public; but the voice of the multitude, or the collective body, is not the *vox populi*. The great
maſs of the people, I have ſhewn, have no political

tical exiftence, their rights in the Conftitution being abforbed by the conftituent Authority; and, by confequence, they have no rights to be confidered as the national opinion to influence the proceedings of Parliament; which indeed can never be influenced but by the wifdom and moderation of the elective body of the people, conftitutionally affembled in their various diftricts.

" We therefore deem it our duty, by every " means which are yet *legal* to appeal to the " judgement of the people, and to procure a de- " claration of their opinion." Can Mr. Fox, who has been fo long acquainted with the principles of our Government, put his hand to his breaft and fay that it is his duty, as a Reprefentative of the People and a Guardian of our Conftitution, to appeal to the judgement of the People at large, who have no political judgement, becaufe they poffefs no right to exercife an opinion but through the channel of the conftituent body? Can the Right Honorable Gentleman, faithful to a great public truft, roufe the great mafs of the people to give an opinion on the conduct of the Legifla- tive and Executive Powers, with which they have nothing to do, and with which they cannot inter- fere without the greateft danger to our Govern- ment? Mr. Fox here miftakes his duty, which

confifts

confifts in explaining in Parliament the true principles of the Conftitution and the true intereft of
the Nation, and not in collecting the opinion of
the Multitude for the rule of his conduct.

" With this view we have invited our fellow
" fubjects to *affociate* for obtaining the repeal of
" two acts paffed in the prefent Seffion of Parliament." In any other man than Mr. Fox this
alarming invitation, upon the principle of the
French Revolution, would denote great ignorance
of our Conftitution and our Law; fince it is manifeftly contrary to the exclufive right of the
conftituent part of the people to affemble in their
feveral diftricts, and in violation of the faid acts
made for the prevention of fuch unneceffary, unconftitutional, and dangerous Affociations; tending to roufe the paffions and prejudices of the
Public againft the neceffary and well-judged meafures of Government, and, by confequence, againft
the peace and fecurity of the Nation.

But fuppofing the Law objected to was really
" repugnant to the genius and character of this
free Nation," Mr. Fox certainly takes the moft
illegal, unconftitutional, and ineffectual method to
procure the repeal, which fhould be effected
through the proper application and well-weighed
opinion

opinion of the real Public, and not from the interefted motives of Party, or the ftrong paffions of the Multitude, which will never have any weight with a wife Government.

Mr. Fox fays " the ruling principle of our " Conftitution is the right of the people to mani- " feft their opinions on great public concerns " without which the forms of a free Conftitution " are worthlefs." It is indeed a great, a glorious principle of a free people to manifeft their opinions on civil Liberty, but it is the wifeft principle of our Conftitution to confide the exercife of that right, on the meafures of Government, to that part of the people called the conftituent body, who are the Reprefentatives of the great body of the public, It would therefore be as unconftitutional as illegal for any other part of the People to manifeft their opinions on the meafures of His Majefty's Minifters, in whom the Public at large place all the confidence that is due to the virtues and wifdom of the Sovereign, and a better than the prefent never reigned to deferve that confidence of the Nation.

" No human wifdom can provide a fafe-guard " againft a *poffible combination of all the branches of* " *the Legiflature to opprefs or betray this Country,*

" but

" but by enabling the great body of the Nation
" freely to pronounce their opinions on the acts
" and meafures of Government." " A *poffible*
" Combination of the whole Legiflature to op-
" prefs and betray the Nation" is as uncharitable
and malicious as a pofitive combination would
be monftrous, fince there does not exift even
the fhadow or the probability of fuch a confede-
racy, oppreffion, and treachery. God forbid there
fhould be the color of truth in " a combination
" of all the branches of the Legiflature to op-
" prefs and betray my Country !" Bad indeed
muft be the heart of that man who can conceive
fuch an unjuft Idea, and cruel muft be the charge
when coming from fuch an authority as Mr. Fox,
to corrupt the minds of a deluded Multitude and
arm their head-ftrong paffions againft His Majefty's Government and againft the peace, the
profperity and fecurity of the Nation. But had
fuch a heavy charge againft " *all* the branches of
" the Legiflature," that of His Majefty not excepted, any exiftence, the Conftitution points
out a better, a fafer, and more effectual method
than a dangerous appeal, like that of France, to
the great mafs of the people to reform the Government.

" The great Statefmen and Lawyers, who
" framed

" framed the DECLARATION of RIGHTS; when
" they afferted the right of the people to petition,
" did, by a neceffary implication, alfo affert
" their right of *affembling* to confider fuch matters
" as might legally be the fubject of petition."
On this vague paffage is grounded all the error
of Mr. Fox's doctrine, to hood-wink the people, and all the delufion of his Adherents. The
right which the Public derive from the Conftitution, as explained by the Bill of Rights, is no
other than what is compatible with the Conftitution itfelf; that is, the right of the conftituent
body *only* to petition the Parliament and the
King, as the head of Executive Government. The
Whig Club would be a Society of Idiots could
they fuppofe that the right of *petitioning* and
affembling was not confined to the conftituent power, but extended, like the univerfal fuffrage of
the Duke of Richmond, to the great mafs of the
people; a principle that would tend to the fubverfion of the Conftitution and the total overthrow of our Government.

It would introduce the reign of anarchy and
confufion with the principles of robbery, injuf-
ftice, and affaffination, which have arifen from
the horrid fyftem of France, upon the ruin of our
mild, beneficent, and juft Government. The
right

right of affembling is eftablifhed upon the very fame foundation as the right of petitioning: the principle that admits the one implies the other. And as the one is contracted, fo is the other; by a tacit furrender of the rights of the collective body to the conftituent part of the People, for the wife purpofes of Legiflation, and for the general purpofes of the Nation at large. This is one of the wifeft principles of our Conftitution, becaufe it is a barrier againft the influence of anarchy and confufion. The People have equal rights to the bleffings of their Conftitution and Laws, and are univerfally reprefented. But to guard againft the calamity of difcord and confufion, the great Mafs of the People tacitly, as a great and glorious principle of the Conftitution, furrender their rights to the Conftituent Body, who have an exclufive right of *electing*, of *petitioning*, and of *affembling*, at at the periods and in the manner, too long eftab- lifhed, and too well known to be repeated. Here then is a refutation of all the falfe claims of popu- lar rights arifing from Mr. Fox's falfe conftruc- tion of the Conftitution.

" We do not affirm that general principles are
" neceffary in any degree to give way to the exi-
" gency of circumftances. But we affert that the
" right of difcuffion and remonftrance is fo ef-
" tial to the Conftitution that it cannot be
" contracted

" controuled or reftrained without a furrender of
" the conftitution itfelf." This I readily admit,
with this great diftinction; that " the difcuffion
" and remónftrance" do not come unconftitution-
ally and illegally from the great body of the People, to fhake Government to its foundation ; but
conftitutionally and legally from the conftituent
body, to which the general right is wifely furren-
dered, as a fecurity againft popular phrenzy,
and the dangerous paffions of an ungovernable
multitude.

" We do not admit that the delinquency of in-
" dividuals ought to work a forfeiture of the liber-
" ties of a nation." I am of the fame opinion,
and fo I fuppofe are His Majefty's Minifters. It
was never, I believe, intended by them to produce
that effect. But I admit that the delinquency of in-
dividuals, at a dangerous period, ought to work on
the wifdom of Government to provide a fecurity
againft it, to prevent its becoming general, to fubvert our Conftitution, by which we fhould forfeit
the liberty, the profperity, and happinefs we now
enjoy under our excellent Government. And hence
I maintain that Executive Government may, for
a time, encroach fomewhat on the rights of
the fubject, when it does not arife from a defign
to increafe the influence of the Crown, but with a

manifeft

manifeſt view to the preſervation of our Government and all the bleſſings we enjoy under it, by the beſt ſecurity of the liberties of the Nation. *Salus populi ſuprema lex.* Every man ſhould, upon an emergency, ſacrifice ſomewhat of his liberty to preſerve the general intereſt, or the happineſs and ſecurity of the whole.

To conclude: I never met with a production ſo unintereſting and impoſing on the credulity of the public, and ſo unworthy of the conſtitutional knowledge and brilliant talents of Mr. Fox, as the "Declaration of the Whig-Club" with his name to it as Chairman. It is a rhapſody fitter for the ſtage, than either the ſenate or the public. It is not to be put in competition with the excellent Pamphlet entitled " Thoughts on " the Engliſh Government," which is the ableſt defence of our Government, and the happieſt refutation of every word that has been advanced by Mr. Fox. The Author of that well-judged and well-timed production, merits the thanks of the Nation; and a diſtinction from His Majeſty, for maintaining the true principles of his Government; while the Whig-Club deſerve, at this intereſting period, the ſtrongeſt reprobation for violating the Conſtitution and the Law, by a general invitation to rouſe the great maſs of the public.

public, and arm their paffions and prejudices againſt the Legiſlative and Executive powers of the Nation, to reduce this happy Country to the unhappy ſituation of France, which the Author of " Thoughts on the Engliſh Government" has virtuouſly endeavored to prevent, by a judicious and well-timed appeal, not to the paffions of the head-ſtrong multitude, but to " the quiet GOOD " SENSE of a ſpirited Nation," by which he ſhews, with great modeſty and perſpicuity, that the beauty of the Conſtitution confiſts in giving to His Majeſty's Government their confidence and affiſtance to promote the beſt meaſures for their profperity and fecurity, and not in the alarming doctrines of party-men, to harrafs Government by an abufe of liberty, to alienate the affections of His Majeſty's fubjects from the wifdom of his reign, and from the true principles of the Conſtitution.

As this APPENDIX is written in a great hurry, I hope the good intention of the Author will plead his excufe with a candid and liberal Public. I am perhaps the more entitled to excufe, as I write from the pureſt motives, totally uninfluenced by every confideration but thofe of truth and pub-lic virtue. I profefs myfelf a conſtitutional and difintereſted writer, totally unconnected with men

c   in

in power, and with party. I mean no defence of Minifters, but what arifes from the neceffity and the goodnefs of their meafures in general. Influenced by a regard for the Conftitution, that is, the true principles of our mild Government, I am neceffarily an enemy to thofe who, for party purpofes, undermine it by the delufion of falfe principles and groundlefs pretences. I am a volunteer in the defence of facred truth and in the fervice of my country. No man has lefs reafon than myfelf to be an advocate for the prefent Adminiftration. But as I never, for a moment, put my own intereft in competition with that of the Public, fo I am zealous for all Minifters who, like the prefent, ably and happily promote the true principles of Government and the true intereft of the nation.

Mine are indeed humble labours, but they have the merit of fincerity and difinterestednefs. I afk no reward for the beft intentions, to affift Executive Government at a period extremely alarming, nor to this country alone, but to all Europe, from the contagion of French principles; which, but for the wifdom of the beft of Sovereigns, and the unfhaken refolution of His Minifters, would have plunged every European Government in the dreadful calamity, which has convulfed and rent that unhappy country. If in any paf-

fage

fage of this production, the liberality of my com-
patriots, fhould think that I merit commendation
for my zeal, modefty requires me to fay, that if in
any thing I fhine, it is with borrowed light. The
little merit that I may poffefs, is reflected from the
great merit of the Author of Thoughts on the
Englifh Conftitution, to whofe fuperior claims on
the munificence of his amiable Sovereign, and the
liberality of his Country, I bow with reverence;
and for whofe eminent fervices to the Nation in
the worft times, fo candidly confeffed in Parliament, I have the greateft confidence that the unjuft defign of a profecution will be changed to
the interpofition of Minifters, that an honourable
mark of His Majefty's approbation may be con-
ferred on him, as an encouragement to that writer, and an example to others, to ftem the tide
of popular delufion that poifons the minds of
the multitude, alienates their affections, and arms
their paffions with refiftance, to convulfe the Nation and overthrow His Majefty's Government.

This modeft wifh arifes from a fenfe of his
great merit, im many important inftances, and
of the great juftice of minifters to their able and
active Friend; totally difinterefted on my part, as
I have not the leaft knowledge of the Gentleman who is fuppofed to be the Author of that
invaluable production, which I think ought to

be

be written in characters of Gold; while that of Mr. Fox claims our pity for the perversion of our Constitution and the abuse of his splendid Talents for the worst of all purposes, namely, that of throwing great obstacles in the way of His Majesty's Government.

Much as I admire the splendid Talents of the Right Honorable Gentleman, and highly as I respect the public opinion in his favor, I am so much alarmed at the mischievous tendency of his rash and unnecessary conduct in the present situation of our domestic and foreign affairs, that, were I in the Commission of the Peace for Middlesex, I should not hesitate a moment to make Mr. Fox amenable to the judicial authority for " seditiously stirring up the people to " resist the measures of Government, in viola- " tion of the Constitution, which has given an " exclusive right to the Constituent part of the " Nation, and in breach of the Peace." As we wisely guard against the apprehension of the Pestilence of the Body Natural, so the same wisdom teaches the necessity of the earliest precaution against the Contagion of the Body Politic. In the one case as in the other, there should be no respect of persons: The greater the power of infusing the poison the greater the reason for its prevention.

prevention. The unfounded and peſtilent conduct of Mr. Fox, the Duke of Bedford, and Mr.
Erſkine in particular, deſerve the earlieſt and
ſevereſt reprehenſion of the Judicial Authority,
to ſtop the torrent of deluſion, and to prevent
effects too dreadful to be deſcribed from the
poiſon of this Political Contagion.

January 30, 1796.

F I N I S.

www.ingramcontent.com/pod-product-compliance
Lightning Source LLC
Chambersburg PA
CBHW020550270326
41927CB00006B/784